SAML 2.0

James Relington

DEDICATION

This book is dedicated to all the professionals working tirelessly to secure digital identities and protect organizations from ever-evolving threats. To the cybersecurity teams, IT administrators, and identity management experts who ensure safe and seamless access for users— your work is invaluable. And to my family and friends, whose support and encouragement made this journey possible, thank you.

AKNOWLEDGEMENTS

I would like to express my deepest gratitude to everyone who contributed to the creation of this book. To my colleagues and mentors in the cybersecurity and identity management field, your insights and expertise have been invaluable. To the organizations and professionals who shared their experiences and best practices, your contributions have enriched this work. A special thanks to my family and friends for their unwavering support and encouragement throughout this journey. Finally, to the readers, thank you for your interest in identity lifecycle management—may this book help you navigate the evolving landscape of digital security with confidence.

Chapter 1: Introduction to SAML 2.0

Security Assertion Markup Language (SAML) 2.0 is a widely adopted open standard that facilitates the exchange of authentication and authorization information between parties, specifically between an identity provider (IdP) and a service provider (SP). Developed by the OASIS consortium and released in 2005, SAML 2.0 has become a cornerstone of federated identity management, enabling Single Sign-On (SSO) across different domains and organizations. The protocol is particularly popular in enterprise environments, where users need seamless access to multiple applications without the hassle of logging in separately to each one.

At its core, SAML 2.0 addresses a fundamental challenge in the digital world: how to securely verify a user's identity across different systems and organizations without requiring them to create and manage multiple sets of credentials. In traditional models, each application or service maintained its own user database, requiring users to remember numerous usernames and passwords. This approach not only created a poor user experience but also increased security risks, as users tended to reuse passwords or choose weak ones. SAML 2.0 resolves this by enabling federated authentication, where a trusted identity provider handles the authentication process and issues assertions to service providers, confirming the user's identity.

A key feature of SAML 2.0 is Single Sign-On (SSO), which allows users to authenticate once with an identity provider and gain access to multiple service providers without needing to log in again. For example, an employee might log in to their company's central authentication portal in the morning and then seamlessly access email, human resources systems, and project management tools throughout the day without additional logins. This not only streamlines the user experience but also reduces the administrative burden on IT departments, which no longer need to manage separate login credentials for each application.

SAML 2.0 operates through a series of standardized components that facilitate secure communication between identity and service providers. The most critical of these components is the assertion, an XML-based message issued by the identity provider that contains information about the authenticated user. Assertions include details such as the user's identity, attributes (like email or role), and any relevant permissions. These assertions are digitally signed to ensure their authenticity and integrity, preventing tampering or forgery.

Another important aspect of SAML 2.0 is its protocols, which define how requests and responses are exchanged between parties. For example, when a user attempts to access a service provider, the service provider sends an authentication request to the identity provider. The identity provider then authenticates the user—typically via username and password or multi-factor authentication—and returns an authentication response containing the assertion. This entire process happens behind the scenes, often in a matter of seconds, providing a seamless experience for the user.

To ensure that these communications are secure and compatible across different systems, SAML 2.0 uses bindings to define how messages are transported. The most common binding is HTTP Redirect, where authentication requests are sent via URL parameters, and HTTP POST, where responses are sent through form submissions. These bindings leverage existing web protocols to facilitate secure and efficient message exchange.

An essential component of SAML 2.0 is metadata, which contains the configuration details necessary for identity providers and service providers to communicate securely. Metadata includes information like public keys for signature verification, endpoints for sending requests and responses, and supported bindings and protocols. By exchanging metadata, parties can establish trust relationships and ensure that their SAML transactions are secure and interoperable.

The architecture of SAML 2.0 supports a wide range of use cases beyond basic Single Sign-On. For example, Single Logout (SLO) is a feature that allows users to log out from all connected service providers with a single action. This is particularly useful in enterprise environments where security policies require comprehensive session termination to prevent unauthorized access. Additionally, SAML 2.0 can facilitate attribute sharing, where identity providers send specific user attributes to service providers to enable personalized experiences or access control based on user roles.

SAML 2.0 has been widely adopted across industries and sectors, from government and education to healthcare and finance. Its ability to provide secure, federated authentication has made it a preferred choice for organizations that need to integrate with multiple third-party services or provide seamless access to cloud-based applications. Many popular enterprise applications, such as Salesforce, Google Workspace, and Microsoft 365, support SAML 2.0 for authentication, making it a critical component of modern IT infrastructure.

Despite its many advantages, SAML 2.0 is not without its challenges. One of the primary criticisms is its complexity, particularly in the initial setup and configuration. The XML-based assertions, metadata exchanges, and digital signatures require a thorough understanding of both the protocol and the underlying security mechanisms. Misconfigurations can lead to vulnerabilities, such as man-in-the-middle attacks or assertion forgery, which can compromise the security of the entire system. To mitigate these risks, organizations must follow best practices for SAML implementation, including regular audits, secure key management, and rigorous testing.

Another challenge with SAML 2.0 is its limited support for mobile applications. While SAML works well in traditional web-based environments, its reliance on browser redirects and form submissions can be cumbersome in mobile contexts. This has led to the rise of alternative protocols like OAuth 2.0 and OpenID Connect, which offer more lightweight, flexible solutions for mobile and API-based authentication. However, SAML remains the standard for many enterprise applications, particularly those that require robust security and federated identity management.

As the digital landscape continues to evolve, the role of SAML 2.0 in identity management remains significant. While newer protocols offer alternatives for specific use cases, SAML's ability to provide secure, federated authentication across diverse environments ensures its continued relevance. Organizations often adopt a hybrid approach, leveraging SAML for enterprise SSO while using protocols like OAuth 2.0 for mobile and API access. This flexibility allows organizations to meet the diverse needs of their users while maintaining a consistent, secure identity management strategy.

SAML 2.0 represents a critical milestone in the evolution of digital identity management. By enabling secure, federated authentication and Single Sign-On, it has transformed how users interact with digital services and how organizations manage access to their resources. Its widespread adoption across industries highlights its effectiveness, while its integration with modern technologies ensures that it will remain a foundational component of identity systems for years to come. As organizations continue to navigate the complexities of digital transformation, SAML 2.0 provides a robust, secure framework for managing identities in an increasingly interconnected world.

Chapter 2: The Evolution of Federated Identity

The concept of federated identity has emerged as a response to the growing complexity of managing user authentication across multiple systems, organizations, and platforms. In the early days of digital authentication, identity management was a straightforward process. Users had individual accounts for each service they accessed, each requiring a separate username and password. This worked well in isolated environments but quickly became unmanageable as users needed to interact with multiple applications, both within and outside of their organizations. The need for a more scalable, secure, and user-friendly authentication model led to the development of federated identity systems.

The first stage in the evolution of identity management was the introduction of centralized directories. Organizations implemented directory services such as Microsoft Active Directory and LDAP-based systems, which allowed user credentials to be stored and managed in a central location. While this approach improved efficiency within a single organization, it did not solve the problem of authentication across different organizations or external services. Users still had to create separate accounts for third-party applications, leading to password fatigue and increased security risks.

As businesses and government entities began collaborating more frequently, the need for cross-organizational authentication became apparent. Early solutions involved trust agreements where organizations manually created accounts for external users, but this was inefficient and insecure. It also required constant maintenance, as users frequently changed roles or left organizations, leading to outdated and unmanageable identity records. The demand for a more dynamic and automated approach to authentication led to the development of federated identity management.

Federated identity allows a user to authenticate once with a trusted identity provider (IdP) and then access multiple service providers (SPs) without needing to reauthenticate. This is accomplished through trust relationships between entities, enabling the secure exchange of authentication and authorization information. The foundational concept behind federated identity is that one organization or entity can vouch for a user's identity, allowing other organizations to accept that authentication without requiring a separate login process.

One of the earliest implementations of federated identity was based on Kerberos, a network authentication protocol developed at MIT. Kerberos introduced the idea of a ticket-based authentication system, where users could obtain a ticket from a trusted authority and present it to multiple services without revealing their password repeatedly. While Kerberos worked well within closed enterprise environments, it was not designed for internet-scale identity federation, leading to the development of more flexible solutions.

As the internet expanded and web applications became the primary way users accessed services, the need for an internet-compatible federated identity standard became critical. The first major effort to address this came in the form of SAML (Security Assertion Markup Language), which provided a standardized way to exchange authentication and authorization information using XML-based assertions. Introduced by the OASIS consortium, SAML enabled identity providers to issue authentication statements that could be consumed by service providers, allowing users to move seamlessly between applications without logging in multiple times.

SAML 2.0, released in 2005, significantly improved the capabilities of federated identity by introducing features like Single Sign-On (SSO), which allowed users to authenticate once and gain access to multiple services. This eliminated the need for repetitive logins and improved the overall user experience while maintaining strong security controls. SAML quickly gained adoption in enterprises, government agencies, and higher education institutions, where users frequently needed to interact with various external applications securely.

As cloud computing and software-as-a-service (SaaS) applications became more prevalent, federated identity continued to evolve. The rise of cloud services required more lightweight and flexible authentication mechanisms that could work across different devices and environments. This led to the emergence of OAuth (Open Authorization), an authorization framework designed to allow secure access delegation. Unlike SAML, which focuses on authentication, OAuth provides a way for applications to grant limited access to user data without exposing credentials.

Building on OAuth, OpenID Connect (OIDC) emerged as a modern authentication protocol that combined the best aspects of OAuth and SAML. OpenID Connect provided an identity layer on top of OAuth 2.0, allowing identity providers to authenticate users and issue JSON Web Tokens (JWTs) that could be used by service providers. This shift towards token-based authentication enabled more seamless interactions between mobile applications, APIs, and cloud services, further advancing the federated identity model.

Another significant development in federated identity is the concept of decentralized identity, where users have greater control over their own identity data. Traditional federated identity systems still rely on centralized identity providers, such as corporate directories or social login services (Google, Facebook, Microsoft). However, decentralized identity initiatives, such as those based on blockchain and self-sovereign identity (SSI), aim to remove the dependency on central authorities by allowing users to store and manage their own identity credentials. This approach enhances privacy and security while maintaining the benefits of federated authentication.

As federated identity continues to evolve, new challenges and opportunities emerge. Security remains a top concern, as federated authentication introduces the risk of identity provider compromise— if an IdP is breached, attackers can gain access to multiple services. To mitigate this risk, organizations adopt multi-factor authentication

(MFA) and continuous authentication mechanisms, which add additional layers of security beyond traditional username-password logins.

Regulatory compliance is another important factor influencing federated identity. Regulations like GDPR (General Data Protection Regulation) and CCPA (California Consumer Privacy Act) require organizations to implement strict data protection measures when handling user identities across borders. Federated identity systems must balance security, privacy, and compliance while providing a seamless user experience.

The increasing adoption of cloud computing, remote work, and digital services continues to drive the evolution of federated identity. Organizations are moving towards hybrid identity models that combine on-premise identity management with cloud-based authentication, ensuring flexibility and security in a rapidly changing landscape. Future developments may further integrate artificial intelligence and machine learning to enhance identity verification, fraud detection, and adaptive authentication.

Federated identity has transformed the way users authenticate and interact with digital services, making authentication more seamless, scalable, and secure. From centralized directories to SAML, OAuth, OpenID Connect, and decentralized identity solutions, the journey of federated identity continues to shape the future of digital authentication. As organizations navigate an increasingly interconnected world, federated identity will remain a fundamental component of secure and efficient access management.

Chapter 3: Core Concepts of SAML

Security Assertion Markup Language (SAML) is an open standard designed to facilitate the secure exchange of authentication and authorization information between parties, particularly between an identity provider (IdP) and a service provider (SP). As organizations increasingly rely on web-based applications and cloud services, SAML plays a crucial role in enabling Single Sign-On (SSO) and federated identity management. To understand how SAML operates and why it has become a cornerstone of modern authentication systems, it is essential to explore its core concepts, including assertions, protocols, bindings, and metadata.

At the heart of SAML is the assertion, an XML-based document issued by an identity provider that conveys information about a user to a service provider. Assertions are the fundamental building blocks of SAML, as they contain the data necessary for service providers to make authentication and authorization decisions. A SAML assertion typically includes three types of statements: authentication statements, attribute statements, and authorization decision statements.

An authentication statement indicates that the user has been authenticated by the identity provider and includes details such as the time of authentication and the method used (e.g., password, multi-factor authentication). This information allows the service provider to trust that the user's identity has been verified by a trusted authority. Attribute statements provide additional information about the user, such as their name, email address, role, or other attributes relevant to the service provider. These attributes can be used to personalize the user experience or enforce access control policies. Authorization decision statements specify whether the user is permitted to access a particular resource, although this type of statement is less commonly used in practice, as authorization is often handled separately by the service provider.

To facilitate the exchange of assertions, SAML defines a set of protocols that outline how requests and responses are communicated between identity providers and service providers. The most important of these is the Authentication Request Protocol, which allows a service provider to request authentication from an identity provider. When a user attempts to access a service, the service provider generates a SAML authentication request and redirects the user to the identity provider. The identity provider then authenticates the user and generates an authentication response containing the assertion, which is sent back to the service provider.

In addition to the Authentication Request Protocol, SAML includes protocols for Single Logout (SLO) and Artifact Resolution. Single Logout enables users to log out from all connected service providers simultaneously after ending their session with the identity provider. This is particularly useful in enterprise environments where users may be logged into multiple applications at once. The Artifact Resolution Protocol, on the other hand, allows service providers to retrieve assertions indirectly using a reference called an artifact, rather than transmitting the full assertion through the browser. This can enhance security by keeping sensitive information off the client side.

SAML also defines bindings, which specify how protocol messages are transported between identity providers and service providers. The most commonly used bindings are HTTP Redirect, HTTP POST, and HTTP Artifact. In the HTTP Redirect binding, the service provider sends the authentication request to the identity provider via a URL query string, redirecting the user's browser. The HTTP POST binding is used to send assertions from the identity provider to the service provider, with the assertion embedded in an HTML form that is automatically submitted by the user's browser. The HTTP Artifact binding allows the service provider to retrieve the assertion from the identity provider using a reference artifact, rather than transmitting the assertion directly through the browser.

A critical component of SAML is metadata, which describes the configuration and capabilities of identity providers and service providers. Metadata includes information such as endpoints for sending requests and responses, public keys for verifying digital signatures, supported bindings and protocols, and organizational details. By exchanging metadata, identity providers and service providers can establish trust relationships and ensure that their SAML transactions are secure and interoperable. Metadata simplifies the configuration process by providing all the necessary information for secure communication in a standardized format.

One of the defining features of SAML is its ability to support Single Sign-On (SSO), which allows users to authenticate once with an identity provider and access multiple service providers without needing to log in again. SSO enhances the user experience by reducing the number of times users need to enter their credentials and improves security by minimizing the risk of password fatigue and weak passwords. In a typical SSO flow, the user attempts to access a service provider, which redirects them to the identity provider for authentication. Once authenticated, the identity provider issues a SAML assertion that is sent back to the service provider, granting the user access to the requested resource. If the user subsequently accesses another service provider within the same federation, the process is repeated without requiring the user to re-enter their credentials.

Another important aspect of SAML is federated identity management, which enables organizations to extend authentication across different domains and organizational boundaries. In a federated identity system, multiple organizations form trust relationships, allowing users from one organization to access resources in another without needing separate credentials. This is particularly useful in scenarios where businesses collaborate with partners, suppliers, or customers, as it simplifies access management and enhances security. SAML facilitates federated identity by providing a standardized framework for exchanging authentication and authorization information across different domains.

Security is a core consideration in SAML, and the protocol includes several mechanisms to ensure the integrity and confidentiality of the information exchanged. Digital signatures are used to verify the authenticity of SAML assertions and messages, ensuring that they have not been tampered with in transit. Encryption is used to protect sensitive information, such as user attributes, from unauthorized access. SAML also includes mechanisms for auditing and logging, allowing organizations to track authentication events and detect potential security incidents.

While SAML offers many benefits, it is not without its challenges. The protocol's reliance on XML and complex configurations can make it difficult to implement and troubleshoot, particularly for organizations without specialized expertise. Misconfigurations can lead to vulnerabilities, such as assertion spoofing or man-in-the-middle attacks, which can compromise the security of the system. To mitigate these risks, organizations must follow best practices for SAML implementation, including regular security audits, robust key management, and thorough testing of configurations.

SAML has been widely adopted across industries, from education and healthcare to government and finance, due to its ability to provide secure, federated authentication. Many popular enterprise applications and cloud services, such as Google Workspace, Salesforce, and Microsoft 365, support SAML for authentication, making it a critical component of modern identity management infrastructures. As organizations continue to move towards cloud-based services and remote work environments, the role of SAML in enabling secure, seamless access to digital resources remains essential.

Understanding the core concepts of SAML is fundamental for anyone involved in identity and access management. By facilitating secure, standardized communication between identity providers and service providers, SAML has transformed the way organizations manage authentication and authorization in an increasingly interconnected world. As technology continues to evolve, SAML's foundational principles will continue to influence the development of new identity standards and protocols, ensuring that secure, federated identity remains at the forefront of digital innovation.

Chapter 4: SAML Architecture Overview

The architecture of Security Assertion Markup Language (SAML) is fundamental to understanding how this protocol enables secure, federated authentication and authorization across diverse systems and organizations. SAML's architecture is designed to facilitate the exchange of authentication and authorization information between trusted entities, primarily the identity provider (IdP) and the service provider (SP). By leveraging standardized components and processes, SAML ensures secure and seamless user experiences, particularly in Single Sign-On (SSO) scenarios. This chapter delves into the key components, roles, and processes that define the SAML architecture, providing a comprehensive understanding of how the protocol operates in real-world applications.

At the heart of SAML architecture are three primary entities: the Identity Provider (IdP), the Service Provider (SP), and the User (or Principal). The Identity Provider is responsible for authenticating the user and issuing SAML assertions, which are XML-based documents that confirm the user's identity and convey relevant attributes. The Service Provider, on the other hand, relies on the assertions provided by the Identity Provider to grant the user access to a specific application or service. The User, often referred to as the Principal in SAML terminology, initiates the authentication process by attempting to access a resource provided by the Service Provider.

The interaction between these entities is governed by a series of protocols and bindings that define how authentication requests and responses are exchanged. The process typically begins when a user attempts to access a service hosted by the Service Provider. Recognizing that the user has not yet been authenticated, the Service Provider generates a SAML Authentication Request and redirects the user's browser to the Identity Provider. This redirection is facilitated through one of SAML's bindings, such as HTTP Redirect or HTTP POST, which ensure secure transmission of the authentication request.

Upon receiving the authentication request, the Identity Provider prompts the user to authenticate, typically through credentials like a username and password or, in more secure environments, multi-factor authentication. Once the user's identity is verified, the Identity Provider generates a SAML Assertion. This assertion is a digitally signed XML document that contains authentication information, such as the time of authentication, the authentication method used, and user attributes like name, email, or role within the organization. The digital signature ensures the integrity and authenticity of the assertion, preventing tampering or forgery during transmission.

The Identity Provider then sends the SAML Assertion back to the Service Provider, again using a secure binding like HTTP POST. The user's browser plays a crucial role in this exchange, acting as the intermediary that carries the assertion from the Identity Provider to the Service Provider. Upon receiving the assertion, the Service Provider verifies the digital signature to ensure the assertion's authenticity and checks the included information to make an access decision. If the assertion is valid and the user meets the necessary criteria, the Service Provider grants access to the requested resource, completing the SAML authentication flow.

Central to the SAML architecture is the concept of trust relationships between Identity Providers and Service Providers. These relationships are established through the exchange of metadata, which contains configuration details necessary for secure communication. Metadata includes information such as entity IDs, public keys for verifying digital signatures, supported bindings and protocols, and endpoints for sending and receiving SAML messages. By exchanging metadata, entities in a SAML federation can ensure interoperability and security, as they have all the necessary information to validate assertions and authenticate users.

Another critical component of SAML architecture is the Assertion Consumer Service (ACS), which is an endpoint on the Service Provider responsible for receiving and processing SAML Assertions. When the Identity Provider sends an assertion to the Service Provider, it is directed to the ACS, where it undergoes verification and validation. The ACS ensures that the assertion is correctly formatted, signed by a trusted Identity Provider, and contains valid information before granting the user access to the requested service.

In addition to authentication, SAML architecture supports features like Single Logout (SLO), which allows users to log out from all connected services with a single action. This is achieved through coordinated communication between the Identity Provider and all associated Service Providers, ensuring that user sessions are terminated across the entire federation. The Single Logout process involves sending logout requests and responses between entities, similar to the authentication flow, to ensure that all sessions are properly closed.

The SAML architecture also accommodates attribute sharing, where the Identity Provider includes additional information about the user in the assertion. This can include attributes such as job title, department, or access privileges, which the Service Provider can use to personalize the user experience or enforce fine-grained access control policies. Attribute sharing enhances the flexibility of SAML, allowing organizations to tailor authentication and authorization processes to their specific needs.

Security is a fundamental consideration in SAML architecture, and the protocol incorporates several mechanisms to protect the integrity and confidentiality of the information exchanged. Digital signatures are used to verify the authenticity of SAML assertions and messages, ensuring that they have not been altered in transit. Encryption is employed to protect sensitive information, such as user attributes, from unauthorized access. Additionally, SAML supports auditing and logging capabilities, allowing organizations to monitor authentication events and detect potential security incidents.

While SAML's architecture is robust and secure, it is also complex, requiring careful configuration and management to ensure proper operation. Misconfigurations can lead to vulnerabilities, such as assertion replay attacks, where a valid assertion is intercepted and reused by an attacker to gain unauthorized access. To mitigate these risks, organizations must implement best practices for SAML deployment, including strict validation of assertions, secure management of cryptographic keys, and regular security audits.

The flexibility of SAML architecture allows it to be integrated into a wide range of environments, from traditional on-premises systems to modern cloud-based applications. Many enterprise applications, such as Salesforce, Google Workspace, and Microsoft 365, support SAML for authentication, making it a critical component of identity and access management infrastructures. The protocol's ability to facilitate secure, federated authentication across diverse systems has made it a preferred choice for organizations looking to streamline access management and enhance security.

Despite the rise of newer authentication protocols like OAuth 2.0 and OpenID Connect, which offer more lightweight solutions for mobile and API-based authentication, SAML remains a cornerstone of enterprise identity management. Its comprehensive architecture, focus on security, and support for federated identity make it well-suited for organizations that require robust and scalable authentication solutions.

Understanding the architecture of SAML is essential for anyone involved in designing, implementing, or managing identity and access management systems. By providing a standardized framework for secure communication between Identity Providers and Service Providers, SAML has transformed the way organizations manage authentication and authorization in an increasingly interconnected world. As technology continues to evolve, the principles and structures of SAML architecture will continue to influence the development of new identity standards and protocols, ensuring that secure, federated identity remains at the forefront of digital innovation.

Chapter 5: Understanding Assertions

At the core of Security Assertion Markup Language (SAML) lies the concept of assertions, which are the primary means by which authentication and authorization data are exchanged between identity providers (IdPs) and service providers (SPs). Assertions are structured XML documents that carry the necessary information to verify a user's identity and determine their access rights to specific resources. Understanding how assertions work, their structure, and their role in the SAML framework is crucial to comprehending the overall mechanism of federated identity management.

A SAML assertion is essentially a statement made by an identity provider about a user, which is then consumed by a service provider to make access control decisions. When a user attempts to access a service, the service provider relies on the assertion provided by the identity provider to confirm the user's identity and, if applicable, to obtain additional attributes necessary for authorization. Assertions are digitally signed to ensure their integrity and authenticity, preventing unauthorized modifications or tampering during transmission.

There are three primary types of statements that can be included in a SAML assertion: authentication statements, attribute statements, and authorization decision statements. Each type of statement serves a distinct purpose in the context of identity verification and access control, and together they provide a comprehensive framework for managing user identities in federated environments.

An authentication statement confirms that a user has been successfully authenticated by the identity provider. This statement includes important details such as the authentication method used (e.g., password, two-factor authentication, biometric verification), the timestamp of the authentication event, and the subject of the authentication—typically represented by a unique identifier like a username or user ID. The authentication statement assures the service provider that the user has been verified according to the specified authentication method and at a specific point in time. This information is critical for maintaining the security and validity of the authentication process, as it helps prevent issues like replay attacks, where an old authentication token might be reused maliciously.

Attribute statements provide additional information about the user, often referred to as user attributes. These attributes can include basic information like the user's name and email address, as well as more detailed data such as their role within an organization, department, job title, or specific permissions. Attribute statements enable service providers to customize user experiences and enforce fine-grained access control based on user-specific information. For example, a user with an attribute indicating a managerial role might have access to higher-level administrative functions within an application, while regular employees have more restricted access. The flexibility of attribute statements allows organizations to tailor authentication and authorization processes to their unique requirements.

The third type of statement, the authorization decision statement, indicates whether a user is authorized to access a particular resource or perform a specific action. While this type of statement is less commonly used in practice—since many service providers handle authorization independently—it can be valuable in scenarios where access decisions need to be centralized or standardized across multiple services. The authorization decision statement specifies the resource in question, the action the user intends to perform (such as read, write, or delete), and the decision made by the identity provider (permit or deny). By including this information in the assertion, the identity provider can influence access control policies at the service provider level.

The structure of a SAML assertion is designed to ensure security, flexibility, and interoperability. Assertions are written in XML, a widely used markup language that provides a standardized format for representing structured data. The assertion consists of several key elements, including the Issuer, Subject, Conditions, Statements, and Signature.

The Issuer element identifies the entity that generated the assertion, typically the identity provider. This is crucial for establishing trust, as the service provider needs to verify that the assertion comes from a trusted source. The issuer is usually represented by a unique identifier, such as a URL or a distinguished name, which is included in the assertion metadata.

The Subject element specifies the user for whom the assertion is issued. This includes a NameID element, which uniquely identifies the user, and may also include additional information about the user's authentication context or session. The subject element can also define SubjectConfirmation methods, which specify how the service provider should verify the assertion. For example, the assertion might require the service provider to confirm that the assertion was received through a specific communication channel or that it includes a valid digital signature.

The Conditions element defines the circumstances under which the assertion is valid. This can include constraints such as the validity period (defined by the NotBefore and NotOnOrAfter attributes), which specifies the time window during which the assertion can be accepted. Conditions can also specify audience restrictions, which limit the assertion's use to specific service providers, and one-time use constraints, which prevent the assertion from being reused in subsequent authentication attempts. These conditions play a critical role in preventing security issues like replay attacks and unauthorized assertion reuse.

The Statements element contains the actual authentication, attribute, and authorization decision statements discussed earlier. Each statement type is represented as a separate sub-element within the assertion, and the information included in these statements forms the basis for the service provider's access control decisions.

Finally, the Signature element ensures the integrity and authenticity of the assertion. The identity provider signs the assertion using its private key, and the service provider verifies the signature using the identity provider's public key, which is typically shared through metadata exchange. This cryptographic process guarantees that the assertion has not been altered in transit and that it originates from a trusted source.

In addition to these core elements, SAML assertions can include encrypted sections to protect sensitive information, such as user attributes, from unauthorized access. Encryption ensures that even if an assertion is intercepted during transmission, the sensitive data it contains cannot be read by unauthorized parties. This is particularly important in scenarios where the assertion includes personal information or other confidential data that must be protected in accordance with privacy regulations.

The use of assertions in SAML provides numerous benefits for both users and organizations. Assertions enable Single Sign-On (SSO), allowing users to authenticate once with an identity provider and access multiple service providers without needing to re-enter their credentials. This improves the user experience by reducing the number of login prompts and minimizes the risk of password-related security issues, such as weak or reused passwords. For organizations, assertions simplify identity management by centralizing authentication processes and reducing the administrative burden associated with managing separate credentials for each application.

However, the use of assertions also introduces certain challenges, particularly related to security and interoperability. Misconfigurations in assertion handling can lead to vulnerabilities, such as assertion spoofing or replay attacks, where malicious actors exploit weaknesses in the authentication process to gain unauthorized access. To mitigate these risks, organizations must implement robust security practices, including proper validation of assertions, secure management of cryptographic keys, and regular security audits.

Interoperability is another key consideration, as SAML assertions must be correctly formatted and compatible with the service providers that consume them. The use of standardized XML schemas and metadata exchange helps ensure that assertions are interoperable across different systems and organizations, but differences in implementation can still pose challenges. Organizations must carefully configure their SAML environments to ensure seamless integration and reliable authentication processes.

Understanding assertions is fundamental to leveraging the full potential of SAML for secure, federated identity management. By providing a standardized, secure way to exchange authentication and authorization information, assertions play a critical role in enabling

Single Sign-On, simplifying identity management, and enhancing the security of digital interactions across diverse systems and organizations. As the digital landscape continues to evolve, the principles and mechanisms underlying SAML assertions will remain central to the development of robust, scalable, and secure identity solutions.

Chapter 6: Protocols in SAML 2.0

Security Assertion Markup Language (SAML) 2.0 is built upon a series of protocols that define how authentication and authorization information is exchanged between identity providers (IdPs) and service providers (SPs). These protocols form the backbone of the SAML framework, dictating the flow of requests and responses that enable Single Sign-On (SSO), Single Logout (SLO), and other federated identity functions. Understanding these protocols is essential to grasp how SAML facilitates secure, interoperable, and efficient identity management across diverse systems and organizations.

At its core, SAML 2.0 is designed to solve the problem of securely transmitting authentication data from one party (the identity provider) to another (the service provider). The primary protocol responsible for this is the Authentication Request Protocol, which enables service providers to request authentication from identity providers on behalf of users. When a user attempts to access a resource at a service provider, and they are not yet authenticated, the service provider generates a SAML authentication request. This request is then sent to the identity provider, typically via the user's browser. The identity provider processes this request, authenticates the user, and generates a SAML response containing an assertion that confirms the user's identity. This assertion is sent back to the service provider, allowing the user to access the requested resource without the need for separate login credentials.

The Authentication Request Protocol is fundamental to enabling Single Sign-On (SSO), one of SAML's most widely used features. SSO allows users to authenticate once with an identity provider and gain access to multiple service providers without needing to log in again. The SSO process is initiated when the service provider sends an authentication request to the identity provider, and the identity provider returns an assertion confirming the user's authentication status. This seamless authentication flow enhances user experience, reduces password fatigue, and improves security by minimizing the need for repeated credential entry.

In addition to authentication, SAML 2.0 includes protocols for managing session termination, most notably the Single Logout (SLO) Protocol. SLO allows users to log out from all connected service providers simultaneously by terminating their session with the identity provider. When a user initiates a logout from one service provider, a logout request is sent to the identity provider, which then propagates the logout to all other service providers with active sessions for that user. This coordinated logout process ensures that user sessions are properly closed across the entire federation, reducing the risk of unauthorized access due to forgotten or lingering sessions.

The SLO protocol supports both IdP-initiated and SP-initiated logout flows. In an IdP-initiated logout, the user logs out directly from the identity provider, which then sends logout requests to all associated service providers. In an SP-initiated logout, the user logs out from a specific service provider, which triggers a logout request to the identity provider and subsequently to other service providers. The logout process involves the exchange of logout requests and logout responses, ensuring that all parties acknowledge the session termination.

Another important protocol in SAML 2.0 is the Artifact Resolution Protocol, which provides an alternative method for transmitting SAML assertions between identity providers and service providers. Instead of sending the full assertion directly through the user's browser, the identity provider generates a small reference called an artifact and sends it to the service provider. The service provider then uses the Artifact Resolution Protocol to retrieve the full assertion from the identity provider's Artifact Resolution Service (ARS). This approach enhances security by keeping sensitive assertion data off the client side and transmitting it directly between trusted servers.

The Artifact Resolution Protocol is particularly useful in environments where security requirements are stringent, such as government or financial institutions. By minimizing the exposure of assertions during transmission, the protocol reduces the risk of interception or tampering by malicious actors. Additionally, the use of artifacts can improve performance in certain scenarios, as smaller messages are transmitted through the user's browser, reducing latency and load times.

SAML 2.0 also includes the Name Identifier Management Protocol, which allows identity providers and service providers to manage and update the identifiers used to represent users within the federation. This protocol supports operations such as name identifier creation, modification, and termination, enabling dynamic management of user identifiers as users move between roles, organizations, or service providers. The protocol ensures that identity information remains consistent and up-to-date across the federation, reducing the risk of identity mismatches or unauthorized access due to outdated information.

In addition to these core protocols, SAML 2.0 defines several auxiliary protocols that support advanced functionality and interoperability. The Assertion Query and Request Protocol allows service providers to query identity providers for specific assertions or attributes about a user, enabling dynamic attribute retrieval and fine-grained access control. The Authentication Context Comparison Protocol provides mechanisms for comparing the strength or context of different authentication events, allowing service providers to enforce specific authentication requirements based on the sensitivity of the requested resource.

The operation of these protocols relies on a series of bindings, which specify how SAML messages are transported between identity providers, service providers, and users. Common bindings include HTTP Redirect, HTTP POST, and SOAP. The HTTP Redirect binding is often used for sending authentication requests from service providers to identity providers, leveraging standard URL query parameters to transmit the message. The HTTP POST binding is commonly used for returning assertions from identity providers to service providers, with the assertion embedded in an HTML form that is automatically submitted by the user's browser. The SOAP binding is used for direct, server-to-server communication, such as in the Artifact Resolution Protocol, where sensitive data is exchanged securely between trusted entities.

Security is a critical consideration in the design and implementation of SAML protocols. All SAML messages, including authentication requests, assertions, and logout responses, are typically digitally signed to ensure their integrity and authenticity. Digital signatures prevent unauthorized modifications to SAML messages during transmission and allow service providers to verify that the messages originate from trusted identity providers. In addition to signatures, encryption is often used to protect sensitive information within assertions, such as user attributes or session details. SAML supports both encryption of the entire assertion and encryption of specific elements, providing flexible options for securing sensitive data.

The robust security features of SAML protocols help mitigate common threats such as replay attacks, man-in-the-middle attacks, and assertion forgery. Replay attacks, where an attacker intercepts and reuses a valid SAML assertion, are prevented through mechanisms like timestamps and unique identifiers that ensure assertions are valid only within a specific time window and for a single use. Man-in-the-middle attacks, where an attacker intercepts and alters SAML messages in transit, are mitigated through the use of TLS encryption for transport channels and digital signatures for message integrity. Assertion forgery, where an attacker attempts to create a fake assertion to gain unauthorized access, is prevented through cryptographic validation of signatures and strict audience restrictions that limit the assertion's use to specific, trusted service providers.

Implementing SAML protocols effectively requires careful configuration and management of both identity providers and service providers. Organizations must ensure that metadata exchange is properly conducted, with accurate and up-to-date information about endpoints, supported bindings, and cryptographic keys. Key management is critical to maintaining the security of SAML messages, with regular key rotation and secure storage practices necessary to prevent compromise. Additionally, organizations should conduct regular audits and security assessments to identify and address potential vulnerabilities in their SAML implementations.

While SAML protocols are powerful and flexible, they can also be complex to implement, particularly for organizations without specialized expertise in identity and access management. The XML-based structure of SAML messages, combined with the need for precise configuration of bindings, protocols, and security features, can create challenges for deployment and troubleshooting. However, the benefits of SAML—seamless Single Sign-On, secure federated identity management, and robust interoperability—make it a valuable tool for organizations seeking to streamline authentication processes and enhance security across their digital ecosystems.

SAML 2.0 protocols have become a standard for enterprise authentication, widely adopted across industries and integrated into numerous applications and services. By defining a comprehensive framework for the secure exchange of authentication and authorization information, SAML protocols enable organizations to build trusted identity federations, simplify user access, and protect sensitive resources in an increasingly interconnected world. As digital environments continue to evolve, the principles and protocols of SAML will remain central to the ongoing development of secure, scalable identity management solutions.

Chapter 7: Binding Mechanisms Explained

In the Security Assertion Markup Language (SAML) 2.0 framework, binding mechanisms play a critical role in defining how SAML messages, such as authentication requests and responses, are transmitted between identity providers (IdPs), service providers (SPs), and users. While SAML protocols establish the structure and content of these messages, bindings specify the communication channels and techniques used to securely transfer them. Understanding binding mechanisms is essential for configuring and maintaining a secure, efficient SAML environment, as the choice of binding affects the security, performance, and user experience of the authentication process.

A binding in SAML is essentially a method of mapping SAML protocol messages onto standard communication protocols, such as HTTP or SOAP. These bindings dictate how messages like authentication requests, assertions, and logout responses are packaged and sent across the internet or internal networks. Since SAML is designed to operate in diverse environments, including web applications, cloud services, and enterprise systems, it supports multiple binding mechanisms to accommodate various use cases and technical requirements.

One of the most commonly used bindings in SAML is the HTTP Redirect Binding. This mechanism is typically employed when sending authentication requests from the service provider to the identity provider. In this binding, the SAML message is encoded and appended as a query parameter to the URL, which redirects the user's browser to the identity provider for authentication. The HTTP Redirect Binding is advantageous because it leverages the existing HTTP protocol, making it compatible with virtually all web browsers and infrastructure components. Additionally, it is lightweight and efficient, as the message is transmitted via a simple URL redirect, minimizing the load on servers and reducing latency.

However, the HTTP Redirect Binding has certain limitations, particularly regarding the size of the SAML messages it can handle. Since URLs have length restrictions, especially in older browsers and network components, large SAML messages may exceed these limits, causing errors or truncation. This limitation makes the HTTP Redirect Binding less suitable for transmitting detailed assertions or messages containing numerous attributes. Additionally, while the binding supports message integrity through digital signatures, the exposure of the message in the URL can raise security concerns, as it may be logged in browser histories or server logs.

To address the limitations of the HTTP Redirect Binding, SAML also supports the HTTP POST Binding, which is widely used for returning authentication responses and assertions from the identity provider to the service provider. In this binding, the SAML message is base64-encoded and included as a hidden field in an HTML form. The form is automatically submitted by the user's browser using the HTTP POST method, ensuring that the message is transmitted securely and without size constraints. The HTTP POST Binding is particularly well-suited for transmitting large or complex SAML assertions, as it avoids the length limitations of URL-based communication.

The HTTP POST Binding also enhances security by keeping the SAML message out of the URL, reducing the risk of exposure in browser histories or logs. Furthermore, the binding supports strong security measures, including the use of digital signatures to verify the integrity and authenticity of the message and transport layer security (TLS) to protect the communication channel. These features make the HTTP POST Binding a preferred choice for transmitting sensitive authentication data in secure environments.

Another important binding in the SAML framework is the HTTP Artifact Binding, which offers a hybrid approach to message transmission. Instead of sending the full SAML assertion through the user's browser, the identity provider generates a small, unique reference called an artifact. This artifact is sent to the service provider via the user's browser, typically using a URL redirect or HTTP POST. Upon receiving the artifact, the service provider uses a back-channel communication method, such as the SOAP Binding, to retrieve the full assertion directly from the identity provider.

The HTTP Artifact Binding provides several advantages, particularly in terms of security and performance. By transmitting only a small reference through the user's browser, the binding minimizes the exposure of sensitive data and reduces the risk of interception or tampering. The actual assertion is retrieved through a secure, server-to-server communication channel, which can be protected with strong encryption and mutual authentication. This approach also helps manage large assertions more efficiently, as the full message is not subject to browser or URL size limitations.

However, the HTTP Artifact Binding introduces additional complexity, as it requires the configuration and maintenance of back-channel communication between the identity provider and the service provider. This can involve managing SOAP endpoints, securing the communication channel with TLS, and handling potential network latency or connectivity issues. Despite these challenges, the binding is valuable in scenarios where security requirements are stringent, such as in government or financial institutions, where minimizing the exposure of sensitive data is paramount.

The SOAP Binding itself is a crucial component of SAML, particularly for back-channel communications like those used in the Artifact Resolution Protocol. SOAP (Simple Object Access Protocol) is a well-established protocol for exchanging structured information in web services, and its integration with SAML allows for secure, reliable server-to-server communication. The SOAP Binding is used to transmit SAML messages directly between identity providers and service providers, bypassing the user's browser entirely. This approach enhances security by ensuring that sensitive data is transmitted over encrypted channels and can be authenticated using mutual TLS.

While the SOAP Binding offers strong security and reliability, it is less commonly used for front-channel communications due to its complexity and the overhead associated with SOAP messaging. It is best suited for scenarios where direct, secure communication between trusted servers is required, such as in artifact resolution or advanced federation configurations.

Another binding worth mentioning is the PAOS Binding (Reverse SOAP), which is used in more specialized scenarios, such as enabling SAML in conjunction with certain web services or device-based authentication flows. PAOS allows SAML messages to be exchanged in environments where traditional HTTP bindings may not be feasible, providing additional flexibility for integrating SAML with various technologies and platforms.

Choosing the appropriate binding mechanism for a SAML implementation depends on several factors, including the security requirements, performance considerations, and technical constraints of the environment. For most web-based applications, the combination of HTTP Redirect and HTTP POST Bindings provides a balance of simplicity, compatibility, and security, making it the most common choice for SAML SSO implementations. The HTTP Artifact and SOAP Bindings are valuable in scenarios where enhanced security is needed or where large assertions must be managed efficiently.

Regardless of the binding chosen, securing the SAML communication process is essential. All bindings should be configured to use TLS encryption for protecting data in transit, and digital signatures should be applied to SAML messages to ensure their integrity and authenticity. Proper management of cryptographic keys and certificates is critical, as compromised keys can undermine the entire security framework of the SAML implementation.

Implementing and managing SAML bindings also requires careful attention to interoperability and compatibility. Different service providers and identity providers may support different bindings, and ensuring that all parties in a SAML federation can communicate effectively is essential for seamless authentication. This often involves exchanging metadata that specifies supported bindings, endpoints, and security configurations, allowing entities to establish trust relationships and configure their systems accordingly.

In summary, binding mechanisms in SAML 2.0 are the methods by which protocol messages are securely transmitted between identity providers, service providers, and users. They play a vital role in ensuring that SAML communications are efficient, secure, and compatible with diverse environments and applications. Understanding the strengths and limitations of each binding mechanism is crucial for designing and implementing robust SAML-based identity management solutions that meet the security, performance, and usability needs of modern organizations.

Chapter 8: Metadata and Configuration

In the Security Assertion Markup Language (SAML) 2.0 framework, metadata and configuration play critical roles in ensuring secure and seamless interactions between identity providers (IdPs) and service providers (SPs). Metadata serves as the foundation for establishing trust, defining communication parameters, and simplifying the complex configurations required for federated identity management. Understanding how metadata works, what it contains, and how it is configured is essential for successfully implementing SAML-based authentication systems in any organization.

Metadata in SAML is an XML document that contains all the necessary information for identity providers and service providers to communicate securely and efficiently. It eliminates the need for manual configuration by providing a standardized format that details how each party in a SAML federation operates. This includes specifying endpoints for message exchanges, public keys for digital signature verification, supported bindings and protocols, and various security policies. By exchanging metadata, both identity providers and service providers can automate much of the configuration process, reducing the risk of errors and ensuring consistency across different systems.

A typical SAML metadata file begins with the EntityDescriptor element, which identifies the organization or system participating in the federation. The entityID attribute within this element serves as a unique identifier for the entity, often represented as a URL. This identifier is critical for distinguishing between different identity providers and service providers in larger federations, where multiple entities may be involved in the authentication process.

Within the EntityDescriptor, there are specific roles defined, such as IDPSSODescriptor for identity providers and SPSSODescriptor for service providers. Each of these descriptors contains detailed information about the capabilities and configurations of the respective entity. For identity providers, the IDPSSODescriptor includes the SingleSignOnService element, which specifies the endpoint URL where authentication requests should be sent. It also lists the supported bindings, such as HTTP Redirect or HTTP POST, allowing service providers to determine how to send their requests.

Similarly, the SPSSODescriptor for service providers contains the AssertionConsumerService element, which defines the endpoint where authentication responses and assertions from the identity provider should be delivered. This descriptor also specifies the bindings supported for receiving assertions, ensuring compatibility with the identity provider's configuration. Additionally, the SPSSODescriptor may include the SingleLogoutService element, detailing how logout requests and responses should be handled in Single Logout (SLO) scenarios.

One of the most important aspects of SAML metadata is the inclusion of cryptographic keys for securing message exchanges. The KeyDescriptor element within both the IDPSSODescriptor and SPSSODescriptor contains the public keys used for verifying digital signatures on SAML messages. These keys ensure the integrity and authenticity of the messages, preventing tampering or forgery during transmission. The KeyDescriptor may also include keys for encryption, which are used to protect sensitive data within SAML assertions, such as user attributes or session information.

In addition to defining communication endpoints and security keys, SAML metadata can specify various security policies and requirements. For example, metadata can indicate whether assertions must be signed or encrypted, what authentication methods are supported, and any restrictions on the usage of assertions, such as audience restrictions or time constraints. These policies help ensure that both identity providers and service providers adhere to consistent security standards, reducing the risk of vulnerabilities and misconfigurations.

The process of exchanging and managing metadata is a crucial part of configuring a SAML federation. Typically, identity providers and service providers generate their metadata files and share them with each other to establish trust. This exchange can be done manually, by sending the XML files via secure channels, or automatically, using metadata exchange protocols or federation management tools. Once the metadata is received, it is imported into the respective systems, allowing them to recognize and trust each other for authentication and authorization processes.

Properly configuring and maintaining metadata is essential for the ongoing security and functionality of a SAML deployment. Since metadata contains critical information about communication endpoints and security keys, it must be kept up to date to reflect any changes in the system architecture or security infrastructure. For example, if an identity provider rotates its cryptographic keys, the corresponding metadata must be updated and redistributed to all service providers in the federation to ensure that signatures can still be verified. Similarly, changes to endpoint URLs or supported bindings require metadata updates to prevent disruptions in the authentication process.

Security considerations are paramount when handling SAML metadata. Since metadata includes sensitive information, such as public keys and endpoint URLs, it must be protected from unauthorized access or tampering. While the metadata itself is often publicly accessible to facilitate federation, it should be hosted on secure servers, transmitted over encrypted channels, and verified for integrity before being imported into systems. Some organizations choose to digitally sign their metadata files to provide an additional layer of assurance that the metadata has not been altered in transit.

Metadata can also include information about attribute requirements and attribute mappings. Service providers often need specific user attributes, such as email addresses, roles, or group memberships, to provide personalized services or enforce access control policies. These attribute requirements can be specified in the metadata, allowing identity providers to configure their attribute release policies accordingly. This ensures that the necessary information is included in the SAML assertions sent to the service providers, enabling seamless integration and functionality.

For organizations participating in large federations or multi-tenant environments, managing metadata can become complex. In such scenarios, metadata aggregation tools or federation management platforms can simplify the process by centralizing metadata management and automating updates. These tools can handle tasks such as metadata signing, validation, distribution, and synchronization, ensuring that all entities in the federation have the latest configuration information without manual intervention.

In dynamic federations, where participants frequently join or leave, automated metadata discovery and exchange mechanisms become even more important. Some federations implement metadata feeds or discovery services that allow entities to automatically retrieve and update metadata from trusted sources. This approach enhances scalability and flexibility, allowing federations to grow and evolve without compromising security or requiring extensive manual configuration.

While metadata significantly simplifies the configuration of SAML systems, it is important to regularly audit and review metadata settings to ensure they align with security best practices and organizational policies. Misconfigurations, outdated information, or overly permissive settings can introduce vulnerabilities or operational issues. Regular metadata audits can help identify and address such issues, ensuring that the SAML federation remains secure and functional.

In addition to facilitating secure communication, metadata also plays a role in enhancing interoperability between different systems and vendors. The standardized format of SAML metadata ensures that identity providers and service providers from different organizations, or even different technology stacks, can interact seamlessly. This interoperability is a key strength of SAML, enabling organizations to integrate a wide range of applications and services into their federated identity environments.

For example, an organization might use a cloud-based identity provider to authenticate users for on-premises applications, or integrate third-party services like Salesforce, Google Workspace, or Microsoft 365 into their SSO environment. The exchange of metadata between these diverse systems ensures that all parties can communicate securely and consistently, regardless of their underlying technologies.

Understanding and effectively managing metadata is fundamental to the successful deployment and operation of SAML-based identity management systems. Metadata not only simplifies configuration but also establishes the trust relationships, security policies, and communication parameters that underpin federated authentication and authorization. By ensuring that metadata is accurately configured, securely managed, and regularly updated, organizations can leverage the full potential of SAML to create robust, scalable, and secure identity solutions for their users and applications.

Chapter 8: Metadata and Configuration

In the SAML 2.0 framework, metadata and configuration play a pivotal role in establishing and maintaining secure, efficient, and interoperable communications between identity providers (IdPs) and service providers (SPs). Metadata, in particular, serves as the foundation for automating the complex setup processes involved in federated identity management. It acts as a blueprint that contains all the essential information each party in the SAML federation needs to trust and communicate with one another. Proper configuration, driven by accurate metadata, ensures seamless Single Sign-On (SSO) experiences and robust security measures.

Metadata in SAML is essentially an XML document that outlines the technical and security details of the entities participating in the federation. This includes information about endpoints for sending and receiving SAML messages, the protocols and bindings supported, and the cryptographic keys required for signing and encrypting assertions. By sharing metadata, identity providers and service providers can automate the configuration of their connections, reducing the likelihood of errors and ensuring that both parties are aligned in their expectations and capabilities.

At the heart of a SAML metadata file is the EntityDescriptor element, which serves as a container for all the configuration information related to a specific entity, whether it is an identity provider or a service provider. The entityID attribute within the EntityDescriptor uniquely identifies the entity in the federation. This identifier is often a URL or a URI that distinguishes one entity from another, which is crucial in federations that involve multiple organizations and services.

Within the EntityDescriptor, roles are specified using elements such as IDPSSODescriptor for identity providers and SPSSODescriptor for service providers. These descriptors define the specific functions and capabilities of each entity. For an identity provider, the IDPSSODescriptor includes information about the SingleSignOnService endpoint, where authentication requests from service providers should be sent. It also lists the supported bindings, such as HTTP Redirect or HTTP POST, which indicate the methods by which SAML messages can be transmitted.

For a service provider, the SPSSODescriptor contains the AssertionConsumerService element, specifying the endpoint where the identity provider should send authentication responses and assertions. This element also includes details about the bindings supported for receiving assertions, ensuring compatibility between the identity provider's output and the service provider's input. Additionally, the SPSSODescriptor may include the SingleLogoutService element, which defines how logout requests and responses should be handled to support Single Logout (SLO) functionality across multiple services.

A critical component of SAML metadata is the inclusion of KeyDescriptor elements, which provide the public keys used for securing SAML messages. These keys are essential for verifying the digital signatures on SAML assertions and ensuring that the messages have not been tampered with during transmission. KeyDescriptors may also include keys for encryption, protecting sensitive data within assertions, such as user attributes or session identifiers. By exchanging these cryptographic keys through metadata, identity providers and service providers establish a foundation of trust that underpins the entire SAML federation.

Metadata also specifies various security policies and requirements that govern how SAML messages should be handled. For instance, metadata can indicate whether assertions must be signed or encrypted, which authentication contexts are supported, and any audience restrictions that limit the use of assertions to specific service providers. These policies ensure that both identity providers and service providers adhere to consistent security standards, reducing the risk of misconfigurations that could lead to vulnerabilities.

The process of exchanging and managing metadata is a fundamental part of configuring a SAML federation. Typically, each entity generates its own metadata file and shares it with its federation partners. This exchange can be done manually, by securely sending the XML files, or automatically, using federation management tools or metadata exchange protocols. Once metadata is received, it is imported into the respective systems, allowing them to recognize and trust each other for authentication and authorization purposes.

Maintaining accurate and up-to-date metadata is crucial for the ongoing security and functionality of a SAML implementation. Any changes to an entity's configuration—such as updates to endpoints, modifications to supported bindings, or the rotation of cryptographic keys—must be reflected in the metadata and shared with all federation partners. Failure to update metadata can result in authentication failures, security vulnerabilities, or disrupted services. For example, if an identity provider changes its signing key but does not update its metadata, service providers will be unable to verify the signatures on assertions, leading to authentication errors.

Security is a paramount concern when handling SAML metadata. Since metadata includes sensitive information like public keys and endpoint URLs, it must be protected from unauthorized access and tampering. While metadata is often made publicly accessible to facilitate federation, it should be hosted on secure servers, transmitted over encrypted channels, and validated for integrity before being imported into systems. Some organizations choose to digitally sign their metadata files, providing an additional layer of assurance that the metadata has not been altered in transit.

Metadata can also include information about attribute requirements and attribute mappings. Service providers often need specific user attributes, such as email addresses, group memberships, or roles, to provide personalized services or enforce access control policies. These attribute requirements can be specified in the metadata, allowing identity providers to configure their attribute release policies accordingly. This ensures that the necessary information is included in the SAML assertions sent to service providers, enabling seamless integration and functionality.

In complex federations or multi-tenant environments, managing metadata can become challenging. Organizations participating in large federations, such as higher education consortia or industry alliances, may need to manage metadata for dozens or even hundreds of entities. In these cases, metadata aggregation tools or federation management platforms can help automate the process of collecting, validating, and distributing metadata. These tools simplify metadata management by providing centralized control over metadata updates, ensuring that all federation participants have consistent and up-to-date configuration information.

For dynamic federations where participants frequently join or leave, automated metadata discovery and exchange mechanisms become even more important. Some federations implement metadata feeds or discovery services that allow entities to automatically retrieve and update metadata from trusted sources. This approach enhances the scalability and flexibility of the federation, allowing it to grow and evolve without compromising security or requiring extensive manual intervention.

While metadata simplifies the configuration of SAML systems, it is important to regularly review and audit metadata settings to ensure they align with security best practices and organizational policies. Misconfigurations, outdated information, or overly permissive settings can introduce vulnerabilities or operational issues. Regular metadata audits can help identify and address such issues, ensuring that the SAML federation remains secure and functional.

Metadata also plays a key role in ensuring interoperability between different systems and vendors. The standardized XML format of SAML metadata ensures that identity providers and service providers from different organizations or using different technology stacks can communicate effectively. This interoperability is one of the key strengths of SAML, enabling organizations to integrate a wide range of applications and services into their federated identity environments.

For example, an organization might use an on-premises identity provider to authenticate users for cloud-based applications like Salesforce or Google Workspace. By exchanging metadata with these service providers, the organization can ensure that authentication requests and responses are handled correctly, and that the necessary security policies are enforced. Similarly, third-party service providers can use metadata to understand the authentication requirements and capabilities of the identity providers they interact with, ensuring seamless integration and user experiences.

Understanding and effectively managing metadata is fundamental to the success of any SAML-based identity management system. Metadata not only simplifies the initial configuration process but also ensures the ongoing security and interoperability of the federation. By accurately configuring, securely managing, and regularly updating metadata, organizations can build robust, scalable, and secure SAML implementations that meet their identity management needs and support seamless, secure access to applications and services.

Chapter 9: Identity Providers (IdP) Demystified

In the realm of Security Assertion Markup Language (SAML) and federated identity management, the Identity Provider (IdP) plays a central role. It is the authoritative entity responsible for authenticating users and issuing security assertions that service providers (SPs) rely on to grant access to resources. Understanding the function, configuration, and significance of an Identity Provider is crucial for anyone working with SAML-based authentication systems. The IdP is not just a component of the authentication process; it is the linchpin that ensures secure, seamless, and efficient user experiences across different applications and services.

An Identity Provider is essentially a trusted source that confirms a user's identity. When a user attempts to access a service or application that requires authentication, the service provider redirects the user to the Identity Provider. The IdP then performs the necessary authentication checks, such as verifying the user's credentials through a username and password, multi-factor authentication, or even biometric verification. Once the user's identity is confirmed, the IdP generates a SAML assertion, a digitally signed XML document that contains information about the authenticated user. This assertion is then sent back to the service provider, which uses it to grant the user access to the requested resource.

The core responsibility of an Identity Provider is to handle authentication securely and efficiently. This involves not only verifying the user's identity but also ensuring that the authentication process adheres to the security policies and requirements of both the IdP and the service providers it interacts with. The IdP must support various authentication methods to accommodate different security needs and user preferences. For example, in high-security environments, the IdP might enforce multi-factor authentication, requiring users to provide a second form of verification, such as a one-time password sent to their mobile device or a biometric scan.

In addition to authentication, Identity Providers are also responsible for managing user attributes and identity information. The IdP maintains a directory or database of user profiles, which includes attributes such as names, email addresses, roles, and group memberships. When generating a SAML assertion, the IdP includes relevant attributes that the service provider can use to make authorization decisions or personalize the user experience. For instance, an IdP might include a user's department and role in the assertion, allowing the service provider to tailor the interface or restrict access based on the user's position within the organization.

One of the key features that make Identity Providers essential in modern IT environments is their ability to facilitate Single Sign-On (SSO). SSO allows users to authenticate once with the IdP and then access multiple service providers without needing to log in again. This seamless authentication flow enhances user convenience, reduces password fatigue, and improves overall security by minimizing the number of times users must enter their credentials. The IdP manages the user's session and ensures that subsequent authentication requests from other service providers are handled without additional user intervention.

The configuration of an Identity Provider is a critical aspect of its operation. Setting up an IdP involves several steps, including defining the authentication methods, configuring the user directory, and establishing trust relationships with service providers. Trust is established through the exchange of metadata, which includes information about endpoints, supported bindings, and cryptographic keys. The IdP shares its metadata with service providers, allowing them to verify the authenticity of the assertions they receive. Similarly, the IdP imports metadata from service providers to ensure that it sends assertions to trusted entities.

Security is at the forefront of Identity Provider operations. The IdP must ensure that all communications are secure, that assertions are properly signed and, when necessary, encrypted. Digital signatures are used to verify the integrity and authenticity of SAML assertions, ensuring that they have not been tampered with in transit. Encryption is employed to protect sensitive information within assertions, such as user attributes, from unauthorized access. Additionally, the IdP must implement robust security measures to protect against common threats, such as replay attacks, where an attacker intercepts and reuses a valid assertion to gain unauthorized access.

Identity Providers must also support various SAML bindings and protocols to facilitate communication with service providers. The most common bindings used by IdPs include HTTP Redirect, HTTP POST, and HTTP Artifact. These bindings define how SAML messages, such as authentication requests and assertions, are transmitted between the IdP and SP. The choice of binding affects the security, performance, and user experience of the authentication process, and the IdP must be configured to support the bindings required by its federation partners.

Beyond the technical aspects, Identity Providers play a strategic role in federated identity management. They enable organizations to extend their authentication capabilities across different domains, applications, and even external partners. This is particularly important in today's interconnected world, where businesses collaborate with vendors, customers, and other third parties. By acting as a central authority for authentication, the IdP allows organizations to maintain control over user identities while enabling secure access to a wide range of services.

In many cases, Identity Providers are integrated with existing enterprise identity management systems, such as Microsoft Active Directory, LDAP directories, or cloud-based identity platforms like Azure Active Directory or Okta. This integration allows organizations to leverage their existing user directories and authentication infrastructure while extending SAML-based federated authentication to external applications and services. The IdP acts as a bridge between the internal identity systems and the broader federation, ensuring that users can access resources securely and seamlessly.

Managing an Identity Provider also involves handling lifecycle events related to user identities. This includes provisioning new users, updating user attributes, and deprovisioning users who leave the organization or change roles. The IdP must ensure that these changes are reflected in the SAML assertions it generates, so that service providers receive accurate and up-to-date information. In dynamic environments, automated synchronization between the IdP and the user directory is often implemented to streamline this process and reduce administrative overhead.

The flexibility and scalability of Identity Providers make them suitable for a wide range of use cases, from small organizations to large enterprises and multi-tenant environments. In educational institutions, for example, an IdP can enable students and faculty to access a variety of academic resources with a single login. In healthcare, an IdP can facilitate secure access to patient records and medical applications while ensuring compliance with privacy regulations. In the corporate world, an IdP can streamline access to cloud services, internal applications, and partner systems, enhancing productivity and security.

While Identity Providers offer numerous benefits, they also come with challenges and responsibilities. The complexity of configuring and managing an IdP can be significant, particularly in large federations with many service providers and complex security requirements. Organizations must invest in the necessary expertise and tools to ensure that their IdP is properly configured, secure, and reliable. Regular audits, security assessments, and updates are essential to maintain the integrity of the IdP and the trust relationships it supports.

Another challenge is ensuring interoperability with different service providers, especially in federations that include diverse technologies and standards. While SAML provides a standardized framework for federated identity management, variations in implementation can lead to compatibility issues. Identity Providers must be configured to handle these differences and ensure that SAML assertions are accepted and processed correctly by all service providers in the federation.

In summary, Identity Providers are the cornerstone of SAML-based federated identity management, providing secure authentication, managing user attributes, and enabling Single Sign-On across multiple services and domains. They play a critical role in establishing trust between entities, facilitating seamless user experiences, and ensuring the security and integrity of the authentication process. By understanding the function and configuration of Identity Providers, organizations can leverage the full potential of SAML to create robust, scalable, and secure identity management solutions.

Chapter 10: Service Providers (SP) Fundamentals

In the world of Security Assertion Markup Language (SAML) 2.0, Service Providers (SPs) play an equally important role as Identity Providers (IdPs) in the broader framework of federated identity management. While the IdP is responsible for authenticating users and issuing assertions that confirm their identity, the SP is the entity that consumes these assertions to grant access to applications, resources, or services. Understanding the fundamentals of Service Providers is essential for comprehending how federated authentication systems function, ensuring secure, seamless access to digital resources across diverse platforms and organizations.

A Service Provider is essentially any application, website, or system that relies on external authentication to verify a user's identity. Instead of managing its own authentication processes, the SP delegates this responsibility to a trusted Identity Provider. When a user attempts to access a resource hosted by the SP, the SP redirects the user to the IdP for authentication. Once the IdP verifies the user's identity, it returns a SAML assertion to the SP, which then processes the assertion and grants or denies access based on the information it contains. This delegation of authentication streamlines user management, enhances security, and simplifies the user experience through Single Sign-On (SSO).

The core function of a Service Provider is to consume and validate SAML assertions provided by the IdP. These assertions are XML-based documents that contain important information about the authenticated user, such as their identity, roles, and other attributes relevant to the application or resource. When the SP receives an assertion, it must perform several key steps to ensure that the assertion is valid and trustworthy. First, the SP verifies the digital signature on the assertion to confirm that it was issued by a trusted Identity Provider and has not been tampered with during transmission. This step is critical for maintaining the integrity and security of the authentication process.

After verifying the signature, the SP checks the validity conditions specified in the assertion. These conditions may include timestamps that define the time window during which the assertion is valid, audience restrictions that specify which service providers are authorized to consume the assertion, and one-time use constraints that prevent the assertion from being reused in subsequent authentication attempts. By enforcing these conditions, the SP ensures that the assertion is being used appropriately and within the intended context.

Once the assertion is validated, the SP extracts the user attributes contained within it. These attributes provide additional information about the user that the SP can use to personalize the user experience or enforce access control policies. For example, an assertion might include attributes such as the user's email address, department, role within the organization, or group memberships. The SP uses this information to determine what resources the user can access and what permissions they have within the application. This attribute-based access control allows for fine-grained management of user privileges, enhancing both security and usability.

The configuration of a Service Provider is a critical aspect of its operation within a SAML federation. Setting up an SP involves defining how it interacts with the Identity Provider, specifying the endpoints for receiving SAML assertions, and configuring the security policies that govern assertion validation. The SP's configuration is typically guided by metadata, an XML document that describes the SP's capabilities, supported bindings, and cryptographic keys. This metadata is shared with the Identity Provider to establish trust and ensure that both parties can communicate securely and effectively.

One of the key elements of SP configuration is the Assertion Consumer Service (ACS) endpoint. This is the URL where the Identity Provider sends SAML assertions after authenticating a user. The SP must be configured to listen at this endpoint and process incoming assertions according to the security and validation policies it has defined. The ACS endpoint is specified in the SP's metadata, allowing the IdP to know where to send authentication responses.

In addition to the ACS endpoint, the SP may also define a Single Logout Service (SLO) endpoint to support coordinated logout processes. Single Logout allows users to log out from all connected applications and services with a single action, ensuring that all active sessions are terminated across the federation. When a user initiates a logout from the SP, the SP sends a logout request to the Identity Provider, which then propagates the logout to other service providers with active sessions for that user. This coordinated approach to session management enhances security by reducing the risk of unauthorized access due to lingering sessions.

Service Providers must also be configured to handle various SAML bindings and protocols. The most common bindings used by SPs include HTTP Redirect, HTTP POST, and HTTP Artifact. These bindings define how SAML messages are transmitted between the SP and IdP. For example, the HTTP Redirect binding is often used to send authentication requests from the SP to the IdP, while the HTTP POST binding is commonly used to receive assertions from the IdP. The choice of binding affects the security, performance, and user experience of the authentication process, and the SP must be configured to support the bindings required by its federation partners.

Security is a paramount concern for Service Providers in a SAML federation. The SP must implement robust mechanisms to verify the integrity and authenticity of SAML assertions, protect sensitive data, and prevent common threats such as replay attacks and assertion forgery. Replay attacks occur when an attacker intercepts a valid assertion and attempts to reuse it to gain unauthorized access. To mitigate this risk, the SP enforces timestamp validation and one-time use conditions, ensuring that assertions are only valid for a limited time and cannot be reused.

In addition to validating assertions, the SP must also protect the communication channels used for transmitting SAML messages. This typically involves using Transport Layer Security (TLS) to encrypt data in transit, preventing interception and tampering by unauthorized parties. The SP's metadata includes cryptographic keys that the IdP uses to sign assertions, and the SP uses these keys to verify the signatures on incoming messages. Proper key management is critical to maintaining the security of the SAML federation, and organizations must implement policies for key rotation, storage, and protection.

Service Providers also play a strategic role in enabling Single Sign-On (SSO) across multiple applications and services. By relying on a central Identity Provider for authentication, the SP allows users to access various resources without repeatedly entering their credentials. This seamless authentication flow enhances user convenience, reduces the administrative burden of managing multiple accounts, and improves security by minimizing the risk of password-related issues. The SP manages the user's session and ensures that subsequent authentication requests are handled transparently, providing a consistent and efficient user experience.

In complex federations or multi-tenant environments, managing multiple Service Providers can become challenging. Organizations may need to integrate a wide range of applications, each with its own unique requirements and configurations. To streamline this process, many organizations use federation management tools or identity brokers that centralize the management of SP configurations and automate the exchange of metadata. These tools simplify the process of adding new service providers, updating configurations, and ensuring consistent security policies across the federation.

Service Providers must also ensure interoperability with different Identity Providers and technology stacks. While SAML provides a standardized framework for federated identity management, variations in implementation can lead to compatibility issues. SPs must be configured to handle these differences and ensure that SAML assertions are processed correctly, regardless of the IdP's underlying technology. This often involves testing and validating the SP's configuration with different IdPs to ensure seamless integration.

Beyond the technical aspects, Service Providers contribute to the overall user experience and security posture of an organization's identity management system. By providing secure, efficient, and user-friendly access to applications and resources, SPs play a critical role in supporting business operations, enhancing productivity, and protecting sensitive information. Understanding the fundamentals of Service Providers, from configuration and security to interoperability and session management, is essential for building robust, scalable, and secure SAML-based authentication systems.

Chapter 11: The Authentication Flow

In the context of SAML 2.0, the authentication flow is the sequence of steps that occur when a user attempts to access a service provider (SP) and needs to be authenticated by an identity provider (IdP). This flow is the foundation of federated identity management and Single Sign-On (SSO), enabling users to authenticate once and gain access to multiple applications without re-entering their credentials.

Understanding the authentication flow is critical for implementing and managing SAML-based systems, as it ensures that secure, efficient, and seamless user experiences are achieved.

The authentication flow typically begins when a user attempts to access a resource or application provided by a service provider. This action triggers the service provider to check whether the user has an existing authenticated session. If no session is found, the service provider initiates the authentication process by generating a SAML authentication request. This request is a specially formatted XML message that asks the identity provider to authenticate the user and return an assertion confirming their identity.

Once the authentication request is created, it needs to be transmitted to the identity provider. This is where bindings come into play. The service provider uses a specific binding method, such as HTTP Redirect or HTTP POST, to send the authentication request to the IdP. In the HTTP Redirect binding, the SAML request is encoded and appended to the URL as a query parameter. The user's browser is then redirected to this URL, effectively sending the request to the identity provider. In the HTTP POST binding, the request is embedded in an HTML form that is automatically submitted to the IdP via the user's browser.

When the identity provider receives the authentication request, it first verifies that the request is valid and comes from a trusted service provider. This involves checking the digital signature on the request, if one is present, and ensuring that the request conforms to the expected format and protocol requirements. If the request passes these checks, the identity provider proceeds to authenticate the user.

The authentication process at the identity provider can vary depending on the organization's security policies and the methods supported. Common methods include traditional username and password combinations, but more secure options like multi-factor authentication (MFA), biometric verification, or smart card authentication can also be used. The goal is to confirm the user's identity with a high degree of confidence before proceeding.

Once the user is successfully authenticated, the identity provider generates a SAML assertion. This assertion is a digitally signed XML document that contains information about the user, such as their identity, attributes, and the authentication context (e.g., the method and time of authentication). The digital signature ensures that the assertion cannot be tampered with during transmission and verifies that it originates from a trusted identity provider.

The next step is for the identity provider to send the assertion back to the service provider. Similar to the initial request, this is done using a binding method, most commonly the HTTP POST binding. The assertion is base64-encoded and included as a hidden field in an HTML form, which is automatically submitted by the user's browser to the service provider's Assertion Consumer Service (ACS) endpoint. The ACS is responsible for receiving and processing SAML assertions.

When the service provider receives the assertion, it performs a series of validation steps to ensure the assertion is legitimate and trustworthy. First, the service provider verifies the digital signature to confirm that the assertion was issued by a trusted identity provider and has not been altered. It then checks the assertion's validity conditions, such as timestamps that specify the assertion's expiration time and audience restrictions that ensure the assertion is intended for this particular service provider.

If the assertion passes all validation checks, the service provider extracts the user's information from the assertion. This includes the user's identity and any additional attributes provided by the identity provider. The service provider uses this information to create a session for the user and grant access to the requested resource or application. Depending on the attributes included in the assertion, the service provider may also apply specific access controls or personalize the user experience.

At this point, the user is successfully authenticated and has access to the service provider's resources. If the user attempts to access another service provider within the same federation, the process can be even more seamless. Since the user is already authenticated at the identity provider, subsequent authentication requests from other service providers can be fulfilled without prompting the user to log in again. This is the essence of Single Sign-On (SSO), which enhances user convenience and reduces the need for multiple logins.

While the standard authentication flow is straightforward, there are variations that can occur depending on how the SAML implementation is configured. For example, in an IdP-initiated SSO flow, the process starts at the identity provider rather than the service provider. In this scenario, the user logs in directly to the identity provider's portal, and the IdP then generates and sends a SAML assertion to the service provider, granting the user access without the need for the initial authentication request from the SP.

Another variation is the use of the Artifact Binding, which adds an additional layer of security by separating the transmission of the SAML assertion from the user's browser. Instead of sending the full assertion through the browser, the identity provider sends a small reference called an artifact. The service provider then retrieves the full assertion directly from the identity provider using a secure back-channel communication. This approach minimizes the risk of assertion interception or tampering during transmission.

Security is a critical aspect of the SAML authentication flow. The use of digital signatures, encryption, and secure transport protocols like TLS (Transport Layer Security) ensures that SAML messages are protected from common threats such as man-in-the-middle attacks, replay attacks, and assertion forgery. Replay attacks, where an attacker intercepts and reuses a valid assertion to gain unauthorized access, are mitigated by strict enforcement of timestamps and one-time use conditions on assertions. Additionally, auditing and logging mechanisms are often implemented to track authentication events and detect potential security incidents.

The SAML authentication flow also requires careful management of cryptographic keys and certificates. Identity providers and service providers must securely manage their private keys, regularly rotate them, and ensure that their public keys are accurately shared through metadata. Compromised keys can undermine the entire security of the SAML federation, so organizations must implement robust key management practices.

From a user experience perspective, the SAML authentication flow offers significant benefits by reducing the number of times users need to enter their credentials and providing seamless access to multiple applications. However, achieving this seamless experience requires careful configuration and coordination between identity providers and service providers. Misconfigurations can lead to authentication failures, security vulnerabilities, or degraded performance, so organizations must invest in proper setup, testing, and maintenance of their SAML systems.

In federated environments where multiple organizations collaborate, the SAML authentication flow enables secure cross-domain authentication. For example, a university student can use their campus credentials to access resources provided by external educational platforms or research institutions, all facilitated by the underlying SAML federation. This ability to extend trust across organizational boundaries is one of the key strengths of SAML and highlights the importance of understanding and properly implementing the authentication flow.

The SAML authentication flow represents a powerful mechanism for enabling secure, federated access to digital resources. By understanding the sequence of steps involved—from initiating an authentication request to validating an assertion and granting access— organizations can build robust, scalable, and secure identity management solutions that enhance both security and user convenience.

Chapter 12: Single Sign-On (SSO) with SAML

Single Sign-On (SSO) is one of the most significant advancements in modern identity and access management, and SAML 2.0 is the protocol that has played a pivotal role in making SSO a standard across enterprises, educational institutions, and various industries. SSO allows users to authenticate once and gain access to multiple applications and services without the need to log in separately to each one. This seamless experience enhances user convenience, improves productivity, and strengthens security by reducing password-related vulnerabilities. Understanding how SSO works with SAML requires an exploration of the underlying mechanisms, benefits, challenges, and practical implementations.

At its core, SSO with SAML relies on the concept of federated identity, where authentication responsibilities are centralized through a trusted Identity Provider (IdP). When a user attempts to access a service provided by a Service Provider (SP), the SP defers the authentication process to the IdP. Once the user is authenticated by the IdP, a SAML assertion is issued, confirming the user's identity and possibly including additional attributes like roles or permissions. This assertion is then consumed by the SP, granting the user access without requiring further credential input. The beauty of SSO lies in its ability to extend this process across multiple SPs, allowing users to move between applications and services effortlessly after a single authentication event.

The SSO process begins when a user tries to access an SP. The SP checks if the user has an active session. If no session exists, the SP generates a SAML authentication request and redirects the user's browser to the IdP. This redirection is typically handled using the HTTP Redirect or HTTP POST binding, ensuring secure transmission of the authentication request. The user's browser facilitates this communication, acting as an intermediary between the SP and the IdP.

Upon receiving the authentication request, the IdP prompts the user to log in if they have not already authenticated during the current session. The authentication method used by the IdP can vary depending on the organization's security policies and user preferences. It might be as simple as a username and password or involve more secure methods like multi-factor authentication, biometric verification, or smart card authentication. The flexibility of SAML allows organizations to choose authentication methods that best meet their security and usability requirements.

Once the user's identity is verified, the IdP generates a SAML assertion. This assertion is a digitally signed XML document that includes information about the user, such as their unique identifier, authentication details, and any relevant attributes. The digital signature ensures the integrity and authenticity of the assertion, preventing tampering or forgery during transmission. The assertion is then sent back to the SP via the user's browser, typically using the HTTP POST binding. The SP receives the assertion at its Assertion

Consumer Service (ACS) endpoint, where it is validated to ensure it comes from a trusted IdP and has not been altered.

After successful validation, the SP creates a session for the user and grants access to the requested resource. If the user then attempts to access another SP within the same federation, the process becomes even more seamless. Since the user is already authenticated at the IdP, subsequent authentication requests from other SPs can be fulfilled without prompting the user to log in again. The IdP recognizes the active session and issues new assertions to the additional SPs, allowing the user to navigate between applications effortlessly.

The primary benefit of SSO with SAML is the improved user experience. Users no longer need to remember multiple sets of credentials or repeatedly enter their login information for different applications. This reduction in credential management simplifies the user's interaction with technology and decreases the likelihood of password fatigue, where users might choose weak passwords or reuse the same password across multiple platforms. By minimizing the need for repeated logins, SSO also enhances productivity, allowing users to focus on their work without frequent interruptions.

From a security perspective, SSO with SAML reduces the risk associated with password management. Since users authenticate once through a centralized IdP, the number of times credentials are transmitted across the network is minimized, reducing exposure to potential interception or phishing attacks. Additionally, organizations can enforce stronger authentication policies at the IdP level, such as multi-factor authentication or adaptive authentication, ensuring a higher level of security for all connected applications.

SSO also simplifies administrative tasks related to user management. IT departments can centralize authentication policies and manage user accounts more efficiently. For example, when an employee joins or leaves an organization, their access to multiple applications can be provisioned or deprovisioned from a single point of control at the IdP. This centralized management reduces the complexity and potential errors associated with maintaining separate user accounts for each application, leading to better compliance with security policies and regulatory requirements.

Despite its many advantages, implementing SSO with SAML is not without challenges. The initial setup can be complex, requiring careful configuration of both the IdP and SPs to ensure compatibility and secure communication. Metadata exchange between entities is critical for establishing trust and defining the technical parameters of the federation. Metadata includes information about endpoints, supported bindings, and cryptographic keys used for signing and encrypting assertions. Ensuring that this metadata is accurate and up to date is essential for the proper functioning of the SSO system.

Interoperability between different systems and vendors can also pose challenges. While SAML is a standardized protocol, variations in implementation across different platforms can lead to compatibility issues. Organizations must thoroughly test their SSO configurations to ensure that assertions are correctly processed and that users can authenticate seamlessly across all connected applications. In some cases, custom configurations or additional middleware may be required to bridge gaps between incompatible systems.

Security considerations are paramount in SSO implementations. While SSO reduces the risk associated with password management, it also creates a single point of failure. If the IdP is compromised, an attacker could potentially gain access to all connected SPs. To mitigate this risk, organizations must implement robust security measures at the IdP level, including strong authentication mechanisms, secure key management, regular security audits, and monitoring for suspicious activity. Additionally, SPs should enforce session management policies, such as session timeouts and re-authentication requirements for sensitive actions, to further enhance security.

Another important aspect of SSO with SAML is the user logout process. The Single Logout (SLO) feature allows users to log out from all connected applications simultaneously by terminating their session at the IdP. When a user initiates a logout from one SP, a logout request is sent to the IdP, which then propagates the logout to all other SPs where the user has active sessions. This coordinated logout process ensures that sessions are properly closed across the entire federation, reducing the risk of unauthorized access due to lingering sessions. Implementing SLO can be complex, as it requires careful coordination between the IdP and all SPs, but it is a critical component of a secure SSO environment.

In federated environments where multiple organizations collaborate, SSO with SAML enables secure cross-domain authentication. For instance, a university student can use their campus credentials to access resources provided by external educational platforms or research institutions. Similarly, in the corporate world, employees can use their company credentials to access third-party services like cloud applications, partner portals, or industry consortium resources. This ability to extend trust across organizational boundaries is a powerful feature of SAML-based SSO, fostering collaboration and efficiency while maintaining security.

SSO with SAML also supports various advanced features that enhance flexibility and control. Attribute-based access control (ABAC) allows SPs to make fine-grained access decisions based on the attributes included in the SAML assertion. For example, access to a particular resource might be granted only to users with a specific role or department. Additionally, SAML supports the inclusion of authentication context information, enabling SPs to enforce different security requirements based on the sensitivity of the resource being accessed.

The scalability of SSO with SAML makes it suitable for organizations of all sizes, from small businesses to large enterprises and multi-tenant environments. Whether integrating a few internal applications or managing access across a vast federation of external partners, SAML provides a robust, secure framework for federated authentication. By centralizing authentication and simplifying access management, SSO with SAML helps organizations enhance security, improve user experience, and streamline administrative processes in an increasingly interconnected digital landscape.

Chapter 13: Single Logout (SLO) Process

Single Logout (SLO) is a critical component of federated identity management systems, especially in environments where Single Sign-On (SSO) is implemented using SAML 2.0. While SSO enhances user convenience by allowing seamless access to multiple applications with a single authentication event, it also introduces the challenge of managing session termination across these applications. SLO addresses this challenge by providing a mechanism to ensure that when a user logs out from one application, their sessions are terminated across all connected service providers (SPs) and the identity provider (IdP). This coordinated logout process is essential for maintaining security and ensuring that no residual sessions remain active, potentially exposing sensitive resources.

The fundamental purpose of SLO is to provide users with a consistent and secure way to end their sessions across an entire federated environment. Without SLO, logging out from one application would only terminate the session for that specific service provider, leaving the user authenticated in other connected applications. This fragmented logout behavior can lead to security risks, as users might assume they are fully logged out when, in reality, they still have active sessions elsewhere. SLO ensures that when a user initiates a logout, all sessions tied to that authentication event are properly closed, reducing the risk of unauthorized access.

The SLO process can be initiated by either the service provider or the identity provider. In SP-initiated SLO, the user logs out from one of the service providers, which then communicates with the IdP to propagate the logout request to other SPs. In IdP-initiated SLO, the user logs out directly from the identity provider's interface, and the IdP sends logout requests to all connected service providers. Both approaches rely on the same underlying SAML protocols and bindings to coordinate session termination across the federated environment.

The SLO process begins when a logout request is generated. This request is a SAML message that contains information about the session to be terminated, including the SessionIndex, which uniquely identifies the user's session. The request also includes details about the initiating entity, whether it's the SP or the IdP, and is digitally signed to ensure authenticity and integrity. The logout request is then transmitted to the appropriate entities using one of the supported SAML bindings, such as HTTP Redirect, HTTP POST, or SOAP.

When a service provider receives a logout request, it validates the request by checking the digital signature and verifying that the request originates from a trusted entity. Once the request is validated, the service provider terminates the user's session and sends a logout response back to the initiating entity, confirming that the session has been successfully closed. The process is then repeated for all other service providers in the federation, ensuring that every active session associated with the user is terminated.

The coordination of logout requests and responses can be complex, especially in federations with multiple service providers and varying configurations. The identity provider plays a central role in managing this complexity by maintaining a record of all service providers where the user has active sessions. This record is typically managed through the SessionIndex attribute, which tracks session information across the federation. When an SLO event is initiated, the IdP uses this information to send logout requests to each SP, ensuring comprehensive session termination.

Security is a critical consideration in the SLO process. Since logout requests and responses involve sensitive session information, they must be protected from tampering and unauthorized access. Digital signatures are used to verify the authenticity of SAML messages, ensuring that only trusted entities can initiate or respond to logout events. Additionally, TLS encryption is employed to secure the communication channels, preventing interception of logout messages by malicious actors.

One of the challenges of implementing SLO is handling partial logouts. In some cases, a service provider might be unavailable or fail to process a logout request correctly. When this happens, the user's session at that particular SP remains active, resulting in an incomplete logout. To mitigate this risk, SAML provides mechanisms for logout response handling, allowing the initiating entity to track the status of logout requests and take appropriate actions if a service provider fails to respond. This might include retrying the logout request, notifying the user of the partial logout, or implementing session timeouts to eventually terminate the inactive session.

User experience is another important aspect of the SLO process. A well-implemented SLO system should provide clear feedback to users, indicating that they have successfully logged out from all applications.

This can be achieved through confirmation messages, redirects to a logout confirmation page, or visual indicators in the user interface. Ensuring that users are aware of their logout status helps prevent confusion and reinforces the security of the system.

In federated environments involving multiple organizations or external partners, SLO becomes even more complex. Each service provider may have different configurations, session management policies, and response behaviors. Ensuring interoperability between these diverse entities requires careful planning, testing, and coordination. Organizations must establish trust relationships through the exchange of metadata, which includes information about logout endpoints, supported bindings, and cryptographic keys. Regular audits and testing are essential to verify that all entities in the federation can handle SLO requests correctly and consistently.

In addition to the standard SLO process, SAML supports front-channel and back-channel logout mechanisms. Front-channel logout uses the user's browser to relay logout requests and responses between the identity provider and service providers. This approach is straightforward and easy to implement but can be less reliable if the user closes their browser or navigates away during the logout process. Back-channel logout, on the other hand, involves direct server-to-server communication using the SOAP binding. This method is more secure and reliable, as it does not depend on the user's browser, but it requires more complex configuration and infrastructure.

Organizations implementing SLO must also consider the performance implications of the logout process. Coordinating logout requests across multiple service providers can introduce latency, especially in large federations. To optimize performance, some systems implement asynchronous logout handling, where logout requests are sent in parallel rather than sequentially. This approach reduces the overall time required to complete the logout process but requires careful management to ensure that all responses are properly tracked and handled.

Another consideration is the scalability of the SLO process. As organizations grow and integrate more applications into their federated identity systems, the complexity of managing logout events increases. Implementing centralized session management tools or identity federation platforms can help streamline SLO coordination and provide better visibility into session activity across the federation. These tools can also automate aspects of the logout process, such as retrying failed logout requests or synchronizing session data between entities.

SLO is not just a technical process; it also has significant security and compliance implications. Many regulatory frameworks, such as GDPR and HIPAA, require organizations to implement robust session management practices to protect sensitive data. Ensuring that users can securely and completely log out of all applications is a key component of compliance with these regulations. Organizations must document their SLO processes, conduct regular security assessments, and ensure that their federated identity systems meet the required standards.

In complex federated environments, SLO also plays a role in incident response and access revocation. If an organization detects a security breach or needs to revoke access for a specific user, initiating an SLO event can quickly terminate all active sessions and prevent unauthorized access to resources. This rapid response capability is essential for minimizing the impact of security incidents and protecting sensitive information.

While implementing SLO can be challenging, the benefits it provides in terms of security, user experience, and compliance make it an essential feature of any SAML-based federated identity system. By ensuring that sessions are consistently and securely terminated across all applications, SLO helps organizations maintain control over user access, reduce security risks, and provide a seamless experience for users navigating multiple services.

Chapter 14: Security Considerations in SAML

Security Assertion Markup Language (SAML) 2.0 has become a cornerstone of federated identity management and Single Sign-On (SSO) systems, allowing organizations to securely authenticate users across multiple applications and domains. While SAML offers a robust framework for secure authentication and authorization, its implementation and management introduce several critical security considerations. Understanding these considerations is essential to protect against potential vulnerabilities and ensure the integrity, confidentiality, and availability of identity systems.

At the heart of SAML security is the use of digital signatures. Every SAML assertion, which carries authentication and attribute information, should be signed by the Identity Provider (IdP) to guarantee its authenticity and integrity. The Service Provider (SP) must verify this signature to ensure that the assertion was indeed issued by a trusted IdP and has not been tampered with during transmission. Failure to properly validate digital signatures can expose systems to assertion forgery, where malicious actors craft fake assertions to gain unauthorized access to protected resources. It is essential for SPs to reject unsigned or improperly signed assertions and for IdPs to use strong, up-to-date cryptographic algorithms for signing.

In addition to digital signatures, encryption is a key component of securing SAML communications. While signatures protect the integrity of messages, encryption ensures the confidentiality of sensitive information contained within assertions, such as user attributes and session details. Assertions can be encrypted in their entirety or selectively, depending on the sensitivity of the data and the security requirements of the organization. Both IdPs and SPs must manage their encryption keys carefully, ensuring that private keys are stored securely and that public keys are distributed through trusted channels, such as metadata exchanges.

Transport Layer Security (TLS) is another critical layer of protection in SAML implementations. All communications between the user's browser, the IdP, and the SP should be transmitted over secure HTTPS connections to prevent man-in-the-middle (MITM) attacks. Without TLS, attackers could intercept SAML messages in transit, potentially capturing sensitive information or injecting malicious data. Organizations should enforce strict TLS configurations, using modern protocols and ciphers, and regularly update their certificates to maintain the security of their communication channels.

One of the most significant risks in SAML implementations is the potential for replay attacks. In a replay attack, an attacker intercepts a valid SAML assertion and attempts to reuse it to gain unauthorized access to a service. To mitigate this risk, SAML assertions include timestamps and unique identifiers that define their validity period and ensure they can only be used once. Service Providers must rigorously enforce these constraints, rejecting assertions that are expired or that have already been processed. Additionally, implementing short-lived assertions and regularly rotating session tokens can further reduce the window of opportunity for replay attacks.

Another critical security consideration is the management of session information. Once a user is authenticated via SAML, the SP creates a session that allows continued access without re-authentication. Proper session management practices are essential to prevent unauthorized access if a session token is compromised. This includes implementing session timeouts, automatic session termination after periods of inactivity, and mechanisms for Single Logout (SLO) to ensure that sessions are terminated across all connected applications when a user logs out. Organizations should also consider implementing multi-factor authentication (MFA) at the IdP level to add an additional layer of security to the initial authentication process.

The Audience Restriction condition in SAML assertions is another important security feature that limits the scope of an assertion's validity. This condition specifies which SPs are authorized to consume the assertion, preventing its use by unauthorized entities. Service Providers must verify that the audience specified in the assertion matches their own identifier, rejecting any assertions intended for other services. This mechanism helps prevent assertion misuse in scenarios where multiple SPs are part of the same federation.

Metadata management is a foundational aspect of SAML security. Metadata contains critical information about the entities in a federation, including their endpoints, supported bindings, and cryptographic keys. Properly managing and securing metadata is essential to maintaining trust relationships and ensuring secure communications. Metadata should be exchanged over secure channels, signed to verify its authenticity, and regularly updated to reflect changes in configurations or key rotations. Failure to maintain accurate metadata can lead to trust failures, where entities cannot authenticate each other, or to security breaches, where outdated keys expose systems to attacks.

Another area of concern in SAML implementations is XML-based attacks, such as XML Signature Wrapping (XSW). SAML relies heavily on XML for message formatting, and improperly validated XML structures can be exploited by attackers to manipulate SAML messages without breaking the digital signature. To prevent such attacks, both IdPs and SPs must implement strict XML parsing and validation procedures, ensuring that signatures are verified against the correct parts of the message and that all elements are processed securely. Using secure libraries and regularly updating them to patch known vulnerabilities is essential to protecting against XML-based threats.

Phishing is another threat vector in SAML environments. Attackers may attempt to trick users into disclosing their credentials by redirecting them to fake IdP login pages that mimic legitimate interfaces. To mitigate this risk, organizations should educate users about recognizing phishing attempts and ensure that all authentication pages are protected by strong TLS certificates. Additionally, implementing domain-specific security measures, such as using unique, hard-to-guess IdP URLs and monitoring for suspicious login activities, can help detect and prevent phishing attacks.

Key management is at the core of SAML security. Both IdPs and SPs rely on cryptographic keys for signing and encrypting SAML messages. Proper key management practices include securely storing private keys, regularly rotating keys, and ensuring that public keys are distributed and updated through trusted channels. Compromised keys can undermine the entire SAML federation, allowing attackers to forge assertions or decrypt sensitive information. Organizations should implement robust key management policies, including the use of hardware security modules (HSMs) for key storage and automated systems for key rotation and distribution.

Access control and attribute management are also important considerations in SAML implementations. While SAML assertions provide authentication information, they can also include attributes that define user roles, permissions, and other identity-related data.

Service Providers must carefully manage how these attributes are used to grant access, ensuring that attribute-based access control (ABAC) policies are enforced consistently. This includes validating that attributes are accurate and up-to-date, as well as ensuring that sensitive attributes are protected through encryption and proper access controls.

In federated environments, trust relationships between entities are the foundation of SAML security. Organizations must establish clear policies for federation governance, defining how trust is established, maintained, and revoked when necessary. This includes setting standards for metadata exchange, key management, and security protocols, as well as conducting regular audits and assessments to verify compliance with security policies. In multi-organization federations, it is essential to have clear agreements and communication channels to manage security incidents and coordinate responses.

Regular security testing and auditing are essential to maintaining the integrity of SAML systems. Organizations should conduct penetration testing, vulnerability assessments, and code reviews to identify and address potential weaknesses in their SAML implementations. Monitoring and logging authentication events, including successful and failed login attempts, assertion processing, and logout activities, provide valuable insights into system activity and help detect suspicious behavior. Implementing intrusion detection systems (IDS) and security information and event management (SIEM) solutions can further enhance the ability to monitor and respond to security incidents in real time.

Regulatory compliance is another important consideration for organizations using SAML for identity management. Regulations such as the General Data Protection Regulation (GDPR), Health Insurance Portability and Accountability Act (HIPAA), and California Consumer Privacy Act (CCPA) impose strict requirements on how personal and sensitive data is handled. SAML systems must be designed to protect user data in accordance with these regulations, including ensuring data minimization, user consent, and auditing capabilities to track data access and usage.

While SAML provides a robust framework for secure federated identity management, it is not without challenges and complexities. Ensuring the security of a SAML system requires careful planning, meticulous configuration, and ongoing maintenance. Organizations must invest in the necessary expertise and tools to implement SAML securely, regularly review and update their systems, and stay informed about emerging threats and best practices. By addressing these security considerations, organizations can build and maintain secure, scalable, and efficient SAML-based identity management solutions that protect user data and support seamless access to digital resources.

Chapter 15: Implementing SAML in Web Applications

Implementing SAML (Security Assertion Markup Language) in web applications is a critical step for organizations looking to secure their authentication processes while offering users a seamless Single Sign-On (SSO) experience. SAML allows for federated identity management, enabling web applications to rely on external identity providers (IdPs) to authenticate users. This approach simplifies credential management, enhances security, and streamlines user access across multiple applications and services. Successfully integrating SAML into web applications involves understanding the protocol's components, configuring both service providers (SPs) and identity providers, and ensuring secure communication throughout the authentication process.

The first step in implementing SAML in a web application is understanding the roles of the primary entities involved. The identity provider is responsible for authenticating users and issuing SAML assertions that contain information about the user's identity and attributes. The service provider, which is the web application itself, consumes these assertions to grant access to users without requiring them to authenticate directly within the application. This separation of authentication and service delivery is the foundation of federated identity management, and it allows organizations to centralize their authentication processes while maintaining flexibility in how users access resources.

Configuring the service provider is a crucial part of the SAML implementation process. The web application must be set up to recognize and trust the identity provider, which involves exchanging metadata between the two entities. Metadata is an XML document that describes the configuration and capabilities of the SP and IdP, including endpoints for communication, supported bindings (such as HTTP Redirect or HTTP POST), and cryptographic keys used for signing and encrypting SAML messages. The service provider's metadata must be shared with the identity provider, and vice versa, to establish a trusted relationship and ensure interoperability.

Once the metadata exchange is complete, the service provider must be configured to handle SAML authentication requests and responses. This involves setting up an Assertion Consumer Service (ACS) endpoint within the web application. The ACS is the URL where the identity provider sends SAML assertions after successfully authenticating a user. The service provider must be able to receive these assertions, validate their digital signatures, and extract the user's identity information to create a session within the application. Implementing the ACS often requires integrating SAML libraries or toolkits into the web application's codebase, depending on the programming language and framework being used.

On the identity provider side, configuration involves specifying the service provider as a trusted entity and defining how authentication requests from the SP are handled. The IdP must be set up to recognize the service provider's metadata, which includes details about the ACS endpoint, supported bindings, and cryptographic keys. The identity provider's role is to authenticate the user—typically through credentials like usernames and passwords, multi-factor authentication, or other secure methods—and generate a SAML assertion that confirms the user's identity. This assertion is then signed with the IdP's private key to ensure its integrity and authenticity before being sent to the service provider.

When implementing SAML in web applications, it is essential to understand the flow of the authentication process. The process typically begins when a user attempts to access the web application. If the user is not already authenticated, the service provider generates a SAML authentication request and redirects the user's browser to the identity provider. This request includes information about the service provider and the authentication context required. The identity provider receives the request, prompts the user to authenticate if necessary, and then generates a SAML assertion confirming the user's identity.

The identity provider sends the assertion back to the service provider via the user's browser, usually using the HTTP POST binding. The browser automatically submits the assertion to the ACS endpoint of the web application. Upon receiving the assertion, the service provider verifies the digital signature to ensure that the assertion was issued by a trusted IdP and has not been tampered with during transmission. The SP also checks the validity conditions of the assertion, such as the time window during which it is valid and the audience restriction specifying that the assertion is intended for this specific service provider.

After successfully validating the assertion, the service provider extracts the user's identity and attributes from the assertion and creates a session within the web application. The user is then granted access to the requested resources without needing to enter credentials directly into the application. If the user later attempts to access another service provider within the same federation, the SSO process allows them to do so without re-authenticating, as the identity provider can issue new assertions based on the existing authenticated session.

Security is a critical consideration when implementing SAML in web applications. All SAML messages, including authentication requests and assertions, should be signed to ensure their integrity and authenticity. The service provider must verify these signatures against the identity provider's public key, which is shared through metadata. Additionally, sensitive information within assertions, such as user attributes, should be encrypted to protect it from unauthorized access during transmission. Transport Layer Security (TLS) should be used for all communications between the user's browser, the identity provider, and the service provider to prevent interception and man-in-the-middle attacks.

Proper session management is also essential to maintaining security in SAML-enabled web applications. Once a user is authenticated, the service provider must manage the session securely, implementing features like session timeouts, automatic session termination after periods of inactivity, and mechanisms for Single Logout (SLO). SLO ensures that when a user logs out from one service provider or the identity provider, all active sessions across the federation are terminated, reducing the risk of unauthorized access due to lingering sessions.

Interoperability between the identity provider and service provider is another important aspect of implementing SAML in web applications. While SAML is a standardized protocol, variations in implementation across different platforms and vendors can lead to compatibility issues. To address this, organizations should use widely supported SAML libraries and tools that adhere to the SAML 2.0 specification. Thorough testing is essential to ensure that the service provider can correctly process assertions from the identity provider and that the authentication flow works seamlessly for users.

Scalability is another factor to consider when integrating SAML into web applications. As organizations grow and add more applications to their federated identity systems, the complexity of managing SAML configurations increases. To streamline this process, many organizations use identity federation platforms or identity-as-a-service (IDaaS) providers that centralize the management of SAML configurations and simplify the process of adding new service providers. These platforms often provide user-friendly interfaces for managing metadata, configuring authentication policies, and monitoring authentication events across the federation.

Monitoring and logging are also important components of a secure SAML implementation. Service providers should log all authentication events, including successful and failed login attempts, assertion processing, and logout activities. These logs provide valuable insights into user activity and can help detect potential security incidents or anomalies. Implementing security information and event management (SIEM) solutions can enhance the ability to monitor and respond to security events in real time.

Regular maintenance and updates are essential to keeping SAML implementations secure and functional. Organizations should regularly review and update their SAML configurations, including rotating cryptographic keys, updating metadata, and applying security patches to SAML libraries and tools. Staying informed about emerging security threats and best practices is also critical to maintaining the integrity of the SAML federation.

Implementing SAML in web applications offers numerous benefits, including enhanced security, simplified user access, and streamlined identity management. By centralizing authentication processes through a trusted identity provider, organizations can reduce the burden of managing credentials, improve user experiences, and ensure that access to applications is secure and compliant with organizational policies. While the process of integrating SAML can be complex, careful planning, thorough testing, and adherence to security best practices can ensure a successful and secure implementation that meets the needs of both users and organizations.

Chapter 16: SAML Tokens and Attributes

Security Assertion Markup Language (SAML) is a widely used protocol for enabling federated identity management and Single Sign-On (SSO) across different domains and applications. At the heart of SAML's functionality are tokens and attributes, which are essential components for securely conveying identity information from an identity provider (IdP) to a service provider (SP). Understanding how these tokens and attributes work is crucial for anyone involved in implementing or managing SAML-based authentication systems. They form the backbone of how authentication, authorization, and user information are securely transferred across systems.

A SAML token, often referred to as a SAML assertion, is an XML-based document issued by the identity provider after a successful authentication event. This assertion serves as proof that the user has been authenticated and contains the necessary information for the service provider to grant access to the requested resource. The SAML token is digitally signed by the identity provider to ensure its authenticity and integrity. Service providers rely on these tokens to make informed decisions about whether to allow or deny access to their resources without directly handling user credentials.

SAML assertions are composed of three primary types of statements: authentication statements, attribute statements, and authorization decision statements. Each of these plays a specific role in the token and collectively enables secure and detailed communication of user identity and access rights.

The authentication statement is the core component of the SAML assertion. It provides details about the authentication event, including the method used (such as password, multi-factor authentication, or biometric verification), the timestamp indicating when the authentication occurred, and the identity of the authenticated user. This information assures the service provider that the user has been verified by a trusted authority and that the authentication event meets the required security standards. The authentication statement typically includes a Subject element, which identifies the user, often represented as a unique identifier like an email address, username, or a system-specific ID.

Attribute statements extend the functionality of SAML assertions by including additional information about the user. These attributes can represent a wide range of data, from basic details like the user's full name and email address to more specific information such as organizational roles, department affiliations, or access privileges. Attributes are crucial for enabling attribute-based access control (ABAC), where access to resources is granted or restricted based on the user's attributes rather than just their identity. For example, a user with an attribute indicating a managerial role might have access to administrative features within an application, while a standard user would have limited permissions.

The flexibility of attribute statements allows organizations to tailor authentication and authorization processes to their specific needs. Attributes are defined using name-value pairs, where the name identifies the attribute (e.g., "email" or "role"), and the value represents the specific information (e.g., "user@example.com" or "Administrator"). The identity provider determines which attributes to include in the SAML assertion based on the service provider's requirements, often defined in metadata or through pre-established agreements. This selective sharing of attributes helps maintain privacy and adhere to data minimization principles by ensuring that only necessary information is shared with each service provider.

While authorization decision statements are less commonly used in SAML implementations, they play an important role in certain scenarios. These statements specify whether a user is permitted to access a particular resource or perform a specific action. The authorization decision is made by the identity provider and communicated to the service provider as part of the SAML assertion. This approach can be useful in environments where centralized access control decisions are preferred, although many service providers opt to handle authorization internally using the attributes provided in the assertion.

The structure of a SAML assertion is designed to ensure security, flexibility, and interoperability. Each assertion contains key elements such as the Issuer, which identifies the entity that generated the assertion (typically the identity provider), and the Conditions, which define the circumstances under which the assertion is valid. Conditions may include time constraints (e.g., NotBefore and NotOnOrAfter timestamps) that specify the validity period of the assertion, as well as audience restrictions that limit the assertion's use to specific service providers.

To protect the integrity and confidentiality of SAML tokens and the attributes they contain, SAML employs robust security mechanisms. Digital signatures are used to sign assertions, ensuring that they have not been altered in transit and that they originate from a trusted identity provider. Service providers must verify these signatures using the public keys provided in the identity provider's metadata. Additionally, sensitive attributes within the assertion can be encrypted to prevent unauthorized access, especially when transmitting data over public networks.

The transport of SAML tokens between the identity provider and service provider is facilitated by SAML bindings, such as HTTP POST or HTTP Artifact. In the HTTP POST binding, the SAML assertion is base64-encoded and transmitted via an HTML form that is automatically submitted by the user's browser. In the HTTP Artifact binding, a small reference (artifact) is sent instead of the full assertion, and the service provider retrieves the complete assertion through a secure back-channel communication with the identity provider. Both methods ensure secure and efficient delivery of SAML tokens.

Service providers play a critical role in processing and validating SAML tokens. Upon receiving a SAML assertion, the service provider must first validate the digital signature to ensure the assertion's authenticity. Next, the SP checks the assertion's validity conditions, including timestamps and audience restrictions, to confirm that the assertion is still valid and intended for the specific service provider. Once validated, the SP extracts the attributes from the assertion and uses them to create a user session and enforce access control policies.

The management of attributes within SAML assertions is a key aspect of maintaining secure and efficient identity systems. Identity providers must carefully determine which attributes to include in assertions, balancing the need for detailed user information with privacy and data protection requirements. Service providers, in turn, must implement robust attribute processing and access control mechanisms to ensure that attributes are used appropriately and securely.

In federated environments, where multiple organizations collaborate and share authentication responsibilities, attribute mapping becomes essential. Different organizations may use different naming conventions or formats for attributes, requiring service providers to map incoming attributes to their internal representations. This mapping process ensures that user information is accurately interpreted and used within the service provider's application. Clear communication and standardized attribute definitions between identity providers and service providers are crucial for successful attribute mapping.

Attribute release policies are another important consideration in SAML implementations. These policies define which attributes are shared with specific service providers, based on the principle of least privilege. By limiting the attributes included in assertions to only those necessary for a particular service, organizations can reduce the risk of data exposure and comply with privacy regulations such as the General Data Protection Regulation (GDPR). Identity providers must implement flexible attribute release policies that can be tailored to the needs of different service providers and use cases.

SAML tokens and attributes also play a role in auditing and compliance. Logging the issuance and consumption of SAML assertions provides valuable insights into user authentication activities and helps detect potential security incidents. Service providers should log details such as the identity of the authenticated user, the attributes received, and the outcome of the assertion validation process. These logs can be used for troubleshooting, monitoring, and demonstrating compliance with regulatory requirements.

The use of custom attributes in SAML assertions allows organizations to extend the protocol to meet specific business needs. Custom attributes can include any information relevant to the organization's access control policies or user management processes. For example, an organization might include a custom attribute indicating whether a user has completed mandatory training or holds a specific certification required for accessing certain resources. Service providers can leverage these custom attributes to enforce detailed access control policies and provide personalized user experiences.

Implementing and managing SAML tokens and attributes requires careful planning, secure configuration, and ongoing maintenance. Organizations must ensure that their identity providers and service providers are properly configured to handle SAML assertions securely and efficiently. This includes regular updates to cryptographic keys, metadata, and attribute release policies, as well as continuous monitoring for potential security threats and vulnerabilities.

SAML tokens and attributes are fundamental to enabling secure, federated authentication and authorization in modern web applications and services. By understanding how these components work and implementing best practices for their management and security, organizations can create robust identity systems that enhance security, simplify user access, and support compliance with privacy and data protection regulations.

Chapter 17: Encryption and Signing in SAML

Security Assertion Markup Language (SAML) has become a cornerstone for federated identity management and Single Sign-On (SSO) systems, providing a standardized way for organizations to securely exchange authentication and authorization data across different domains. At the heart of SAML's security framework are two essential components: encryption and digital signing. These cryptographic techniques ensure the confidentiality, integrity, and authenticity of the data transmitted between identity providers (IdPs) and service providers (SPs). Understanding how encryption and signing work in SAML is crucial for anyone implementing or managing SAML-based authentication systems, as they play a pivotal role in protecting sensitive user information and maintaining trust between entities.

Digital signing in SAML serves the primary purpose of ensuring the integrity and authenticity of SAML messages, particularly assertions. When an IdP issues a SAML assertion, it signs the assertion using its private key. This digital signature acts as a seal, verifying that the assertion was indeed created by the trusted IdP and has not been altered in transit. The SP, upon receiving the assertion, uses the IdP's public key—typically shared through metadata—to verify the signature. If the assertion's signature is valid, the SP can trust that the information within the assertion is authentic and untampered.

The process of signing SAML assertions involves several steps. First, the IdP generates the assertion containing information about the authenticated user, such as their identity, roles, and attributes. The assertion is formatted as an XML document, and the IdP uses its private key to apply a digital signature to the assertion. This signature is created using cryptographic algorithms such as RSA-SHA256 or ECDSA-SHA256, which provide strong protection against tampering. The signature is embedded within the XML document in a <ds:Signature> element, which includes information about the signing algorithm, the key used, and the actual signature value.

When the SP receives the signed assertion, it extracts the signature and verifies it using the IdP's public key. This verification process ensures that the assertion has not been modified since it was signed and that it originated from the trusted IdP. If the signature verification fails, the SP rejects the assertion, preventing unauthorized access. This mechanism protects against assertion forgery and man-in-the-middle (MITM) attacks, where an attacker might try to intercept and modify SAML messages.

In addition to signing assertions, SAML allows for the signing of other message types, such as authentication requests and logout requests. Signing these messages provides an additional layer of security by ensuring that all communications between the IdP and SP are authenticated and protected from tampering. For example, when an SP sends an authentication request to the IdP, signing the request allows the IdP to verify that the request originated from a trusted SP and has not been altered in transit.

While digital signing ensures the integrity and authenticity of SAML messages, encryption is used to protect the confidentiality of sensitive information within those messages. In many cases, SAML assertions contain personal or sensitive data, such as user attributes, roles, or session information. To prevent unauthorized access to this data, the assertion—or specific parts of it—can be encrypted before being transmitted to the SP.

The process of encrypting SAML assertions typically involves using the SP's public key, which is shared with the IdP through metadata. When the IdP generates an assertion that contains sensitive information, it encrypts the assertion using the SP's public key. This ensures that only the SP, which holds the corresponding private key, can decrypt and access the contents of the assertion. The encryption process uses robust cryptographic algorithms, such as AES-256 for symmetric encryption and RSA or Elliptic Curve Cryptography (ECC) for key exchange.

SAML supports both full assertion encryption and element-level encryption. In full assertion encryption, the entire SAML assertion is encrypted, ensuring that all information within the assertion is protected from unauthorized access. This approach provides comprehensive confidentiality but requires the SP to decrypt the entire assertion to access any information. In element-level encryption, only specific parts of the assertion, such as sensitive user attributes, are encrypted. This allows the SP to process non-sensitive parts of the assertion without decryption while still protecting sensitive data.

The encrypted data is embedded within the XML document using the <xenc:EncryptedData> element, which specifies the encryption method and contains the encrypted content. The <xenc:EncryptedKey> element is also included, providing the encrypted key information needed for the SP to decrypt the data. When the SP receives the encrypted assertion, it uses its private key to decrypt the encryption key and then decrypts the assertion or specific elements as needed.

Implementing encryption and signing in SAML requires careful configuration and management of cryptographic keys. Both IdPs and SPs must generate, store, and manage their private keys securely, ensuring that they are protected from unauthorized access. Private keys should be stored in secure environments, such as Hardware Security Modules (HSMs) or encrypted key stores, and access should be restricted to authorized personnel. Public keys, on the other hand, are shared through metadata exchanges, allowing trusted entities to verify signatures and encrypt data.

Key management also involves key rotation and revocation processes. Regularly rotating cryptographic keys helps mitigate the risk of key compromise and ensures that the encryption and signing algorithms remain secure over time. When a key is rotated, the new public key must be updated in the metadata shared between the IdP and SP. If a private key is compromised, it must be immediately revoked, and the associated public key must be removed from the metadata to prevent further use.

In addition to managing cryptographic keys, organizations must also ensure that their metadata is accurately configured and securely transmitted. Metadata contains critical information about the endpoints, supported bindings, and cryptographic keys used for signing and encryption. Ensuring that metadata is signed and transmitted over secure channels, such as HTTPS, helps protect against tampering and ensures that entities in the federation can trust the information they receive.

Security best practices recommend using strong, up-to-date cryptographic algorithms for both signing and encryption. Older algorithms, such as SHA-1 or RSA with small key sizes, are considered vulnerable and should be avoided. Organizations should follow current industry standards and guidelines, such as those provided by the National Institute of Standards and Technology (NIST) or the European Union Agency for Cybersecurity (ENISA), to ensure that their cryptographic implementations are robust and resistant to attacks.

While encryption and signing are essential for securing SAML communications, they can also introduce performance overhead. Encrypting and decrypting assertions, as well as verifying digital signatures, require computational resources that can impact the performance of the authentication process. Organizations must balance security and performance by optimizing their cryptographic configurations and ensuring that their infrastructure can handle the additional processing requirements.

Monitoring and auditing are also critical components of managing encryption and signing in SAML. Organizations should log all events related to the issuance, signing, encryption, and validation of SAML assertions, as well as any errors or failures in the process. These logs provide valuable insights into the security and performance of the SAML system and can help detect potential security incidents or misconfigurations. Implementing Security Information and Event Management (SIEM) solutions can enhance the ability to monitor, analyze, and respond to security events in real time.

In federated environments, where multiple organizations collaborate and share authentication responsibilities, establishing and maintaining trust relationships is fundamental. Trust is built on the proper management and exchange of cryptographic keys and metadata. Organizations must establish clear policies for federation governance, defining how keys are managed, how metadata is exchanged, and how trust is established and revoked when necessary. Regular audits and security assessments help ensure that all entities in the federation adhere to these policies and maintain the integrity of the SAML system.

Encryption and signing in SAML are not just technical requirements; they are foundational to the trust and security of federated identity management systems. By ensuring the confidentiality, integrity, and authenticity of SAML messages, these cryptographic techniques protect sensitive user information, prevent unauthorized access, and maintain the trust relationships that enable seamless and secure access to applications and services. Proper implementation, management, and monitoring of encryption and signing are essential for building robust, secure, and compliant SAML-based authentication systems that meet the needs of modern organizations.

Chapter 18: Troubleshooting SAML Errors

When implementing SAML (Security Assertion Markup Language) in an enterprise environment, encountering errors is not uncommon. SAML-based authentication involves a complex interplay between identity providers (IdPs), service providers (SPs), digital signatures, encryption, and metadata configurations. Even small misconfigurations or network issues can lead to authentication failures, causing frustration for users and administrators alike. Effective troubleshooting requires a clear understanding of the typical errors, their underlying causes, and the methods to diagnose and resolve them.

One common category of SAML errors involves problems with digital signatures and certificates. For example, if an SP cannot verify the signature on a SAML assertion, it may reject the authentication attempt. This can occur if the IdP's public key is not correctly uploaded or updated in the SP's metadata. In such cases, administrators should first ensure that the public keys and certificates in the SP and IdP metadata match. Checking the validity dates of certificates is also crucial—expired certificates can cause sudden authentication failures. Administrators can also review logs at the SP and IdP to see if the signature verification process returns any specific error codes, which can help pinpoint the exact cause.

Another frequent issue is related to metadata misalignment. SAML relies heavily on metadata exchanges to establish trust between IdPs and SPs. If either party's metadata is outdated, incorrect, or not properly imported, authentication requests may fail. Common symptoms include receiving errors like "Unknown entity ID" or "Audience restriction not met." To address these issues, administrators should verify that the entity IDs specified in the metadata are correct and match what the IdP and SP expect. Additionally, any changes to endpoints, such as Single Sign-On (SSO) or Single Logout (SLO) URLs, should be reflected in the updated metadata and re-imported on both sides.

Time synchronization problems can also lead to SAML errors. Because SAML assertions often include timestamps and validity windows, even slight clock skew between the IdP and SP can cause assertions to appear invalid. If the SP sees an assertion that appears to be from the future or from the distant past, it will reject it. Administrators should ensure that both systems are using reliable time sources—preferably the same NTP (Network Time Protocol) server—to maintain consistent and accurate time. Checking the time zone settings and verifying that all servers are set to the correct time zone can also prevent these errors.

Binding mismatches are another common culprit. SAML supports multiple bindings, such as HTTP Redirect, HTTP POST, and HTTP Artifact, to transmit SAML messages. If the IdP and SP are configured to use different bindings, the SAML request or response may not be handled correctly. For instance, if the SP expects a response via HTTP POST but the IdP sends it via HTTP Redirect, the authentication will fail. Troubleshooting these issues involves verifying the supported bindings listed in the metadata and ensuring that both parties agree on the binding method for requests and responses. Reviewing network traffic captures or SAML trace logs can help identify if the wrong binding was used.

Attribute mapping errors can also cause unexpected failures. When an IdP sends attributes about a user—such as username, email, or roles—the SP must map these attributes to its internal user schema. If the attribute names or formats differ between the IdP and SP, authentication may appear successful, but the user might not be correctly provisioned or may be denied access. Administrators should carefully review the attribute statements in the SAML assertion and confirm that the SP is configured to correctly interpret and map those attributes. Adjusting the attribute mappings on the SP or adding attribute transformations on the IdP side often resolves these issues.

Single Logout (SLO) errors are another common challenge in SAML environments. If the SLO process fails, users may remain logged in on certain SPs even after they log out from the IdP or another SP. This can happen if one or more SPs do not correctly handle logout requests or if the SLO URLs in the metadata are incorrect. Troubleshooting SLO issues typically involves verifying that the correct SLO endpoints are configured, checking that the SP supports the chosen binding for logout messages, and ensuring that the logout responses are properly signed and validated. Examining logs from the IdP and SP during a logout event can reveal whether the logout request reached its destination or if it was blocked due to a misconfiguration.

Another area to consider when troubleshooting is network-related issues. Firewalls, proxies, and load balancers can sometimes interfere with SAML message flow. For example, if a firewall blocks traffic on certain ports or a load balancer changes the originating IP address of a request, the SAML authentication process may fail. Reviewing network logs, ensuring that the necessary ports are open, and confirming that load balancers are configured to preserve original source IPs can help address these issues. Additionally, using HTTPS is critical to prevent man-in-the-middle attacks and ensure that SAML messages are not intercepted or altered in transit.

Sometimes the errors are due to incorrect configurations in the SAML libraries or tools being used by the SP or IdP. Outdated or improperly configured SAML modules can cause unexpected behavior. If possible, ensure that the software libraries handling SAML requests and responses are up to date and compatible with the SAML version used by both the IdP and SP. Documentation from the SAML vendor or library maintainers often provides guidance on common configuration pitfalls and recommended settings.

When troubleshooting SAML errors, the most valuable resource is often the logs generated by the IdP, SP, and the web servers involved. These logs can provide detailed error messages, stack traces, and timestamps that help narrow down the cause of the problem. Tools such as SAML tracers, browser extensions, or debugging utilities can capture the exact SAML messages exchanged during authentication. By comparing these logs and traces to the expected behavior, administrators can identify where the process is failing and take targeted steps to resolve the issue.

In summary, troubleshooting SAML errors involves a combination of verifying metadata, ensuring correct time synchronization, checking digital signatures and certificates, confirming the use of compatible bindings, and carefully reviewing attribute mappings. By systematically analyzing logs, reviewing configuration settings, and ensuring that all components are aligned, administrators can resolve most common SAML errors and maintain a secure, reliable federated authentication environment.

Chapter 19: SAML vs. Other Identity Standards

In the realm of identity and access management, Security Assertion Markup Language (SAML) has long been a foundational protocol for enabling Single Sign-On (SSO) and federated identity across diverse organizations and applications. However, SAML is not the only standard in this domain. Other identity standards such as OAuth, OpenID Connect (OIDC), and LDAP (Lightweight Directory Access Protocol) offer different approaches to managing authentication and authorization. Understanding how SAML compares to these other standards is crucial for organizations deciding which protocol best fits their security needs, application architecture, and user experience goals.

SAML, introduced in the early 2000s, is an XML-based standard designed primarily for federated authentication. It allows identity providers (IdPs) to issue assertions to service providers (SPs), confirming a user's identity and providing relevant attributes. This enables users to log in once and gain access to multiple applications without re-entering credentials. SAML is widely used in enterprise environments for web-based SSO, particularly in industries like education, government, and large corporations where cross-domain authentication is necessary. Its strength lies in its robust security model, which relies on digital signatures and encryption to protect assertions and ensure their integrity and confidentiality.

In contrast, OAuth is a protocol primarily focused on authorization rather than authentication. OAuth allows users to grant third-party applications limited access to their resources without sharing their credentials. For example, a user can authorize a social media app to access their photo gallery without giving the app their password. OAuth operates using tokens, typically in the form of JSON Web Tokens (JWTs), which represent the permissions granted. These tokens can be scoped to specific resources and have defined lifespans, offering granular control over what third-party applications can do on behalf of the user. While OAuth excels at authorization, it was not originally designed for authenticating users, leading to the development of OpenID Connect.

OpenID Connect (OIDC) builds on top of OAuth 2.0 to provide an authentication layer. By introducing the concept of an ID token, OIDC allows applications to verify the identity of a user in addition to obtaining authorization. The ID token contains information about the authenticated user, such as their unique identifier and attributes like email or name, and is signed by the identity provider. OIDC's reliance on JSON and RESTful APIs makes it well-suited for modern web and mobile applications, offering a lightweight and flexible alternative to SAML. While SAML uses XML and requires more complex configurations, OIDC's JSON-based structure is easier to implement and integrates seamlessly with APIs and microservices architectures.

Another key identity standard is LDAP, which serves as a protocol for accessing and managing directory information. LDAP is commonly used within organizations to manage user credentials and attributes in centralized directories, such as Microsoft Active Directory. While LDAP is not a federated identity protocol like SAML or OIDC, it plays a critical role in identity management by serving as the backend repository for authentication systems. Many SAML and OIDC implementations use LDAP directories as their source of truth for user information, retrieving data from LDAP to populate assertions or tokens.

One of the primary differences between SAML and OIDC lies in their use cases and architectural models. SAML was designed for enterprise SSO in browser-based environments. It excels in scenarios where users access multiple web applications across organizational boundaries, such as logging into various cloud-based services from a corporate identity provider. The XML-based nature of SAML and its reliance on HTTP Redirect or POST bindings make it particularly suited for web browsers, but less flexible for mobile applications and APIs. OIDC, on the other hand, was created with modern web and mobile applications in mind. Its use of RESTful APIs and JSON makes it lightweight and adaptable, ideal for single-page applications (SPAs), mobile apps, and microservices environments.

When considering security features, both SAML and OIDC offer robust mechanisms, but they differ in their implementations. SAML relies heavily on digital signatures and encryption of assertions to protect the integrity and confidentiality of the data being transmitted. Assertions are typically signed by the IdP and verified by the SP to ensure authenticity. OIDC, leveraging OAuth 2.0, uses JWTs (JSON Web Tokens), which are compact, URL-safe tokens that are signed and optionally encrypted. The JWT signature allows the recipient to verify the token's authenticity, while the optional encryption provides confidentiality. OIDC also benefits from fine-grained access control through the use of scopes and claims, which specify the exact information an application can access.

Another area of comparison is the complexity of implementation. SAML's XML structure and strict protocols can make it challenging to implement, especially for developers unfamiliar with XML or the intricacies of SAML bindings. Configuring SAML often involves setting up metadata exchanges between the IdP and SP, configuring certificate-based encryption and signing, and managing complex attribute mappings. OIDC, by contrast, is generally easier to implement due to its use of JSON and RESTful APIs. Developers familiar with modern web development practices find OIDC more intuitive, and many popular frameworks and libraries offer built-in support for OIDC, simplifying integration.

From a performance perspective, OIDC typically has the edge over SAML. The compact size of JWTs and the efficiency of RESTful API calls make OIDC faster and more responsive, particularly in high-traffic environments or applications where speed is critical. SAML assertions, being XML-based, are larger and require more processing power to parse and validate. This difference in performance can be significant in mobile or API-driven applications where lightweight, efficient protocols are preferred.

When evaluating adoption and support, both SAML and OIDC are widely supported but cater to different audiences. SAML is deeply entrenched in enterprise environments, particularly in sectors like education, government, and large corporations where complex federations and cross-domain authentication are common. Many legacy systems and enterprise applications still rely on SAML for SSO. OIDC, on the other hand, has gained traction in modern web and mobile development, with widespread adoption by major technology companies and cloud service providers. Platforms like Google, Microsoft, and Amazon support both protocols but often favor OIDC for their newer services.

OAuth 2.0, while not an authentication protocol on its own, remains the foundation for OIDC and is heavily used for authorization scenarios. It is the standard choice for granting third-party applications access to user resources, such as accessing a user's calendar or files. OAuth's token-based approach provides fine-grained control over what actions an application can perform, and its use of refresh tokens allows for long-term access without repeatedly asking users to authenticate. However, OAuth's flexibility can sometimes lead to security pitfalls if not implemented correctly, as it requires careful handling of tokens and proper configuration of scopes and permissions.

Choosing between SAML, OIDC, and other identity standards depends on the specific needs of the organization and the applications involved. For enterprises with established legacy systems and a strong need for cross-domain SSO, SAML remains a robust and reliable choice. For modern, API-driven applications, mobile apps, and cloud services, OIDC offers a more flexible, lightweight solution that integrates easily with contemporary development practices. In environments where authorization is the primary concern, OAuth 2.0 provides the tools needed to manage access to resources without exposing user credentials.

Ultimately, SAML and other identity standards each have their strengths and weaknesses, and many organizations adopt hybrid approaches to leverage the best features of each protocol. For example, an enterprise might use SAML for internal SSO across legacy systems while adopting OIDC for cloud-based applications and mobile services. Understanding the nuances of each standard allows organizations to build secure, scalable, and user-friendly identity management systems that meet the evolving demands of today's digital landscape.

Chapter 20: Integrating SAML with Cloud Services

As organizations increasingly shift their infrastructure and applications to the cloud, secure and efficient identity management becomes a critical component of their IT strategies. Security Assertion Markup Language (SAML) plays a pivotal role in this transition, offering a standardized framework for enabling Single Sign-On (SSO) and federated identity management across cloud services. By integrating SAML with cloud platforms, organizations can maintain centralized control over user authentication, enhance security, and provide seamless access to multiple cloud applications without requiring users to remember multiple credentials.

Integrating SAML with cloud services begins with understanding the roles of the Identity Provider (IdP) and Service Provider (SP) in the SAML framework. In this model, the IdP is responsible for authenticating users and issuing SAML assertions that confirm their identity. The cloud service, acting as the SP, consumes these assertions to grant access to its resources. This architecture allows organizations to leverage their existing identity infrastructure—such as Active Directory or LDAP directories—to authenticate users while using cloud-based applications like Salesforce, Google Workspace, Microsoft 365, and AWS.

One of the primary benefits of integrating SAML with cloud services is the ability to implement Single Sign-On (SSO) across both on-premises and cloud environments. With SSO, users can authenticate once with their corporate credentials and gain access to a variety of cloud applications without needing to log in separately to each one. This not only improves the user experience by reducing password fatigue but also enhances security by minimizing the risk of password reuse and phishing attacks. By centralizing authentication with a trusted IdP, organizations can enforce consistent security policies, such as multi-factor authentication (MFA) and password complexity requirements, across all connected services.

The integration process typically starts with configuring the cloud service as a Service Provider in the SAML federation. Most cloud platforms provide detailed documentation and support for SAML integration, offering pre-configured options for common IdPs like Azure Active Directory, Okta, and ADFS (Active Directory Federation Services). The cloud service generates metadata, an XML document that describes its SAML configuration, including endpoints for receiving assertions, supported bindings, and public keys for verifying digital signatures. This metadata is shared with the IdP, which uses it to configure trust relationships and determine how to communicate securely with the cloud service.

On the IdP side, administrators configure the cloud service as a trusted SP by importing its metadata and defining policies for issuing SAML assertions. This involves specifying which users or groups are allowed to access the service, what attributes should be included in the assertions, and how those attributes are mapped to the cloud service's user schema. For example, the IdP might include attributes such as the user's email address, display name, department, or role, which the cloud service uses to provision user accounts and enforce access controls. Ensuring that attribute mappings are correctly configured is crucial for seamless integration and proper user provisioning.

Security considerations play a vital role in integrating SAML with cloud services. All SAML assertions should be digitally signed by the IdP to ensure their authenticity and integrity. The cloud service verifies these signatures using the IdP's public key, which is included in the metadata exchange. Additionally, sensitive information within assertions—such as user attributes or session tokens—can be encrypted to protect it from unauthorized access during transmission. Both the IdP and SP must support robust Transport Layer Security (TLS) configurations to secure the communication channels and prevent man-in-the-middle attacks.

Another important aspect of integrating SAML with cloud services is managing user lifecycle events, such as provisioning, de-provisioning, and role changes. While SAML itself is primarily an authentication protocol, it can be extended to support Just-In-Time (JIT) provisioning, where user accounts are created automatically in the cloud service when a user logs in for the first time. This approach simplifies user management by eliminating the need for manual account creation. However, for more comprehensive user lifecycle management, organizations may integrate SAML with SCIM (System for Cross-domain Identity Management), which provides standardized APIs for managing user accounts and attributes across multiple services.

Single Logout (SLO) is another feature that can be implemented when integrating SAML with cloud services. SLO allows users to log out from all connected applications simultaneously by terminating their session at the IdP. When a user initiates a logout from the cloud service, a logout request is sent to the IdP, which propagates the logout to other service providers where the user has active sessions. This coordinated logout process helps maintain security by ensuring that sessions are properly closed across the entire federation, reducing the risk of unauthorized access due to lingering sessions.

Integrating SAML with cloud services also introduces challenges related to interoperability and configuration complexity. Different cloud providers may implement SAML slightly differently, leading to compatibility issues or unexpected behavior. For example, some services may require specific attribute formats, case sensitivity in user identifiers, or unique configurations for SAML bindings. Troubleshooting these issues often involves reviewing detailed logs, capturing SAML assertions using tools like SAML tracers, and ensuring that metadata is accurately configured and up-to-date on both the IdP and SP sides.

Performance considerations should also be addressed when integrating SAML with cloud services. While SAML is a robust and secure protocol, its reliance on XML can introduce processing overhead, particularly in high-traffic environments. Ensuring that the IdP infrastructure is scalable and optimized for performance is critical to maintaining a smooth user experience. Load balancing, redundancy, and efficient session management practices can help mitigate potential performance bottlenecks.

Many organizations adopt hybrid identity models when integrating SAML with cloud services, combining on-premises identity management with cloud-based IdPs or identity brokers. For example, an organization might use Azure Active Directory as a cloud-based IdP while maintaining on-premises Active Directory for local resources. In this model, SAML enables seamless integration between the two environments, allowing users to authenticate with their corporate credentials regardless of whether they are accessing on-premises applications or cloud services.

Federation hubs and identity brokers can further simplify the integration of SAML with multiple cloud services. These platforms act as intermediaries between the IdP and various SPs, centralizing identity management and simplifying the configuration process. By using an identity broker, organizations can manage a single SAML configuration for multiple cloud services, reducing administrative overhead and ensuring consistent security policies across all connected applications. Examples of such platforms include Okta, Ping Identity, and Auth0.

Monitoring and auditing are essential components of a secure SAML integration with cloud services. Organizations should log all authentication events, including successful and failed login attempts, assertion processing, and logout activities. These logs provide valuable insights into user activity, help detect potential security incidents, and support compliance with regulatory requirements. Implementing Security Information and Event Management (SIEM) solutions can enhance the ability to monitor and respond to security events in real time, providing a centralized view of authentication activity across both on-premises and cloud environments.

Compliance and regulatory considerations also play a significant role in integrating SAML with cloud services. Many industries are subject to regulations such as GDPR, HIPAA, and SOX, which impose strict requirements on how user data is handled and protected. SAML helps organizations meet these requirements by providing a secure and standardized method for authenticating users and protecting sensitive information during transmission. Ensuring that SAML assertions are properly signed, encrypted, and audited is critical to maintaining compliance and protecting user privacy.

Integrating SAML with cloud services is a powerful strategy for organizations seeking to streamline identity management, enhance security, and improve user experiences in the cloud. By leveraging SAML's robust framework for federated authentication, organizations can maintain centralized control over user access, enforce consistent security policies, and provide seamless Single Sign-On across a wide range of cloud applications. While the integration process can be complex, careful planning, secure configuration, and ongoing monitoring ensure that SAML-enabled cloud services operate efficiently, securely, and in alignment with organizational goals.

Chapter 21: Common Use Cases for SAML

Security Assertion Markup Language (SAML) is a widely adopted standard that facilitates secure communication of authentication and authorization data between identity providers (IdPs) and service providers (SPs). Since its introduction, SAML has become a cornerstone of identity and access management (IAM), offering solutions to various challenges in enterprise security and user management. The flexibility and security of SAML make it suitable for a broad range of use cases, from Single Sign-On (SSO) to cross-organizational federations, cloud integrations, and regulatory compliance.

One of the most prominent and widely recognized use cases for SAML is Single Sign-On (SSO) within enterprises. SSO allows users to authenticate once using their primary credentials and gain access to multiple applications without needing to log in again. This seamless user experience reduces password fatigue, minimizes the risk of weak password practices, and increases productivity by eliminating the need for repeated logins. In organizations with numerous internal applications—such as email systems, customer relationship management (CRM) tools, and enterprise resource planning (ERP) software—SAML-based SSO simplifies access management and enhances security by centralizing authentication through a trusted IdP.

Cross-domain and cross-organizational federations represent another common use case for SAML. In today's interconnected world, businesses often collaborate with partners, suppliers, and contractors who require access to certain internal systems. SAML facilitates federated identity management, enabling external users to authenticate with their home organization's credentials while gaining access to the host organization's resources. This approach eliminates the need for creating and managing separate accounts for external users, reducing administrative overhead and enhancing security by relying on the external organization's established authentication processes. For example, in the education sector, universities often use SAML to create federations that allow students and faculty from different institutions to access shared research platforms and academic resources.

The rise of cloud computing has further expanded the relevance of SAML. Many cloud service providers, such as Microsoft 365, Google Workspace, Salesforce, and AWS, support SAML for authenticating users through enterprise identity systems. Organizations leveraging multiple cloud applications benefit from SAML by integrating these services with their existing IdPs, providing a unified authentication experience across both on-premises and cloud environments. This not only enhances security by applying consistent policies like multi-factor authentication (MFA) but also simplifies user management through centralized control of access to various cloud platforms.

In the context of government and public sector organizations, SAML is often used to comply with stringent security and privacy regulations. Governments frequently require robust identity management frameworks that can handle sensitive data and enforce strict access controls. SAML's support for digital signatures and encryption ensures the integrity and confidentiality of authentication data, meeting the high security standards necessary in these environments. For example, in the United States, the Federal Identity, Credential, and Access Management (FICAM) program utilizes SAML to facilitate secure federated identity management across federal agencies and external partners.

Healthcare organizations also rely heavily on SAML to meet regulatory requirements such as the Health Insurance Portability and Accountability Act (HIPAA). HIPAA mandates stringent controls over access to electronic protected health information (ePHI), requiring secure authentication methods and audit capabilities. SAML supports these requirements by providing a secure and standardized framework for managing authentication across healthcare systems. Hospitals, clinics, and insurance providers can integrate SAML with their electronic health record (EHR) systems, enabling healthcare professionals to access patient data securely while maintaining compliance with privacy regulations.

In the financial services sector, SAML plays a crucial role in securing access to sensitive financial information and complying with industry regulations such as the Payment Card Industry Data Security Standard (PCI DSS). Banks, investment firms, and payment processors use SAML to implement SSO and federated identity management across their internal systems and customer-facing applications. By centralizing authentication and applying consistent security policies, financial institutions can reduce the risk of data breaches and ensure that access to sensitive data is tightly controlled.

SAML is also widely used in educational institutions, where students, faculty, and staff need access to a variety of online resources, including learning management systems (LMS), library databases, and collaboration tools. Educational federations, such as eduGAIN in Europe and InCommon in the United States, leverage SAML to create a network of trusted identity providers and service providers across multiple institutions. This enables users to access shared academic resources with their institutional credentials, fostering collaboration and simplifying access management across universities and research organizations.

Another important use case for SAML is in customer identity and access management (CIAM), where organizations need to authenticate external users, such as customers, partners, or suppliers. While protocols like OpenID Connect (OIDC) and OAuth 2.0 are often used in consumer-facing applications, SAML remains a viable option for B2B scenarios where federated identity is required. For instance, a software vendor offering a SaaS product might integrate SAML to allow corporate customers to authenticate their employees using their internal identity systems. This approach streamlines onboarding, enhances security by leveraging the customer's authentication infrastructure, and provides a seamless user experience.

Regulatory compliance is another domain where SAML demonstrates its value. Many industries are subject to regulations that require strong authentication, secure data transmission, and detailed audit logs. SAML's support for digital signatures, encryption, and standardized logging helps organizations meet these requirements. For example, the General Data Protection Regulation (GDPR) in the European Union mandates strict controls over personal data, including how user identities are managed and protected. SAML's robust security features ensure that authentication data is handled securely, helping organizations comply with GDPR and other privacy regulations.

SAML is also instrumental in facilitating mergers and acquisitions (M&A). When two companies merge or one acquires another, integrating disparate IT systems and identity management processes can be challenging. SAML provides a standardized way to federate identities across the combined organizations, allowing users from both entities to access shared resources without the need for complex migrations or duplicative account management. By establishing trust relationships between the IdPs and SPs of the merging companies, SAML enables seamless access to applications and resources during the integration process.

In the technology sector, SAML is commonly used to integrate third-party applications and services with enterprise identity systems. Many software vendors provide SAML support in their products, allowing customers to integrate these applications into their existing SSO infrastructure. This not only simplifies user access but also enhances security by ensuring that all applications adhere to the same authentication policies. For example, integrating SAML with developer tools, project management platforms, or HR systems allows organizations to streamline access management and enforce consistent security standards across their technology stack.

Remote work and telecommuting have further amplified the importance of SAML in modern organizations. As more employees access corporate resources from outside traditional office environments, secure and efficient authentication mechanisms are critical. SAML enables remote workers to authenticate using their enterprise credentials and gain access to cloud-based applications, virtual private networks (VPNs), and other resources without compromising security. By centralizing authentication through a trusted IdP, organizations can apply security measures like MFA and conditional access policies, ensuring that remote access is both secure and user-friendly.

SAML is also useful in multi-tenant environments, where a single application serves multiple organizations or groups. In such scenarios, SAML allows each tenant to use its own identity provider for authentication, while the service provider handles authorization and resource management. This is particularly common in SaaS applications, where different customers need to authenticate their users using their internal identity systems. SAML facilitates this by providing a flexible and secure framework for managing authentication across multiple tenants without compromising security or user experience.

As organizations continue to embrace digital transformation, SAML remains a foundational technology for secure identity and access management. Whether enabling SSO in large enterprises, supporting cross-organizational federations, securing cloud applications, or ensuring compliance with regulatory requirements, SAML provides a versatile and robust solution. Its ability to integrate with a wide range of applications and environments makes it a critical component of modern identity management strategies, ensuring that users can access the resources they need securely and efficiently.

Chapter 22: Setting Up a Simple SAML Environment

Setting up a simple SAML environment involves configuring an Identity Provider (IdP) and a Service Provider (SP) to securely exchange authentication information. This setup allows users to authenticate through a central authority (the IdP) and access multiple services (the SPs) without needing to re-enter credentials. While SAML configurations can become complex in large-scale enterprise environments, the basic principles remain consistent and can be implemented in smaller, controlled environments to gain familiarity with the protocol.

The first step in setting up a SAML environment is selecting the software or platforms that will serve as the Identity Provider and Service Provider. Many open-source and commercial solutions are available for both roles. For the IdP, popular options include Shibboleth IdP, SimpleSAMLphp, and Keycloak. On the SP side, applications like Shibboleth SP, SimpleSAMLphp, or even third-party SaaS applications that support SAML can be configured. For this example, we will focus on using SimpleSAMLphp for both the IdP and SP roles due to its ease of setup and comprehensive documentation.

Once the software is selected, the next step is to install SimpleSAMLphp. This application is a PHP-based SAML toolkit that simplifies the process of configuring SAML environments. To begin, you need a server with PHP and a web server like Apache or Nginx installed. After downloading the SimpleSAMLphp package from its official website, extract the contents to your web server's root directory. This will create a directory structure that includes configuration files, metadata templates, and the administrative interface.

With the software installed, the next phase involves configuring the Identity Provider. Navigate to the config directory within the SimpleSAMLphp installation and locate the config.php file. This file contains the core settings for the application, including paths, security settings, and administrative credentials. Set the baseurlpath to point to the URL where SimpleSAMLphp will be accessible. Additionally, create a strong administrative password for accessing the web interface.

Next, configure the Identity Provider settings by editing the authsources.php file in the same directory. Here, you will define how the IdP authenticates users. For a simple environment, you can use the example-userpass module provided by SimpleSAMLphp, which allows for hardcoded username and password combinations. This setup is suitable for testing purposes but should be replaced with a more secure authentication backend, such as LDAP or Active Directory, in production environments. Define users in the example-userpass array, assigning usernames, passwords, and attributes like email or role.

Once the IdP is configured, the next step is setting up the Service Provider. On a separate server or in a different directory on the same server, install another instance of SimpleSAMLphp to act as the SP. The config.php file for the SP should be edited to point to its base URL, and the administrative credentials should be set up for managing the SP interface. The most critical part of SP configuration is defining the IdP that it will trust for authentication.

To establish trust between the IdP and SP, you need to exchange metadata. Metadata is an XML document that describes the configuration and capabilities of each party, including endpoints for communication, supported bindings, and cryptographic keys. In the SimpleSAMLphp interface, you can generate metadata for both the IdP and SP. Export the IdP's metadata and import it into the SP's metadata/saml20-idp-remote.php file. Similarly, export the SP's metadata and import it into the IdP's metadata/saml20-sp-remote.php file. This exchange ensures that both parties recognize and trust each other for secure communication.

Once the metadata exchange is complete, configure the SP's authsources.php file to define how it will authenticate users via the IdP. Specify the IdP's entity ID and ensure that the bindings (such as HTTP-POST or HTTP-Redirect) match those supported by both parties. With these settings in place, the SP is ready to send authentication requests to the IdP and receive assertions in return.

To enhance security, configure digital signatures and encryption for SAML assertions. In the IdP's configuration files, enable signing for assertions and specify the private key to be used. The corresponding public key should be included in the metadata shared with the SP, allowing it to verify the authenticity of the assertions it receives. Similarly, if sensitive user attributes are being transmitted, enable encryption in the IdP settings and ensure that the SP's public key is used to encrypt the assertions.

Testing the setup is the next critical step. SimpleSAMLphp provides a web-based interface for testing SAML authentication flows. Navigate to the SP's SimpleSAMLphp interface and select the option to test authentication. This will initiate a SAML authentication request, redirecting you to the IdP's login page. Enter the credentials defined in the IdP's example-userpass configuration. If the setup is correct, you will be authenticated, and the SP will display the SAML attributes received from the IdP.

If errors occur during testing, review the logs generated by SimpleSAMLphp. These logs provide detailed information about authentication requests, responses, and any errors encountered. Common issues include metadata mismatches, incorrect endpoint URLs, or problems with digital signatures. Ensuring that both the IdP and SP have accurate and up-to-date metadata is often the key to resolving these issues. Additionally, verifying that both parties support the same bindings and protocols is essential for successful communication.

Once basic authentication is functioning correctly, consider enhancing the environment with additional features like Single Logout (SLO) and attribute mapping. SLO allows users to log out from all connected applications simultaneously, improving security and user experience. Configure SLO endpoints in both the IdP and SP metadata, and test the logout process to ensure that sessions are properly terminated. Attribute mapping involves defining how user attributes from the IdP are interpreted by the SP. This can be configured in the SP's settings to ensure that attributes like roles, departments, or permissions are correctly applied within the application.

For environments that require multi-factor authentication (MFA), SimpleSAMLphp can be extended with plugins or integrated with external MFA providers. This adds an additional layer of security by requiring users to provide a second form of verification, such as a one-time password or biometric authentication, in addition to their primary credentials.

Maintaining a secure and reliable SAML environment requires ongoing monitoring and maintenance. Regularly review logs for unusual activity, update software to address security vulnerabilities, and rotate cryptographic keys periodically to maintain security. As the environment grows, consider scaling the IdP infrastructure to handle increased authentication requests and integrating additional service providers into the federation.

Setting up a simple SAML environment provides valuable insights into how federated authentication works and lays the foundation for more complex identity management solutions. By understanding the core components and processes involved, administrators can confidently expand their SAML implementations to support a wide range of applications and services, ensuring secure and efficient access to resources across their organizations.

Chapter 23: Advanced SAML Configuration Techniques

As organizations scale and diversify their IT environments, the need for more sophisticated and secure identity management systems becomes apparent. While basic SAML configurations cover essential use cases such as Single Sign-On (SSO) and simple federations, advanced SAML configuration techniques offer greater flexibility, security, and interoperability across complex infrastructures. Mastering these advanced techniques allows organizations to fine-tune their identity management processes, integrate with diverse applications, and address specific security and compliance requirements.

One of the most critical advanced techniques in SAML configuration is fine-grained attribute mapping and transformation. In basic SAML setups, identity providers (IdPs) pass user attributes like email, username, and roles to service providers (SPs) without much modification. However, in more complex environments, attributes often need to be transformed to meet the specific requirements of different service providers. For instance, an SP might require roles to be formatted in a particular way or expect custom attributes that are not natively available in the IdP. Attribute transformation involves using scripting or policy rules within the IdP to manipulate and map attributes before they are included in the SAML assertion. This ensures that the SP receives exactly the data it needs, formatted appropriately, to grant access or apply specific permissions.

Another advanced configuration is implementing multi-factor authentication (MFA) at the IdP level. While many organizations use MFA for direct logins, integrating MFA into the SAML authentication flow provides an additional layer of security across all federated applications. This involves configuring the IdP to enforce MFA policies based on specific criteria, such as user roles, group memberships, or the sensitivity of the requested service. For example, users accessing financial applications might be required to complete an additional verification step, such as a one-time password (OTP) sent to their mobile device, while users accessing less sensitive applications might only require standard credentials. This contextual MFA approach enhances security while maintaining a balance with user convenience.

Conditional access policies represent another layer of sophistication in SAML configurations. These policies enable organizations to control access based on contextual factors like geographic location, device type, time of access, or IP address ranges. By integrating conditional access into the SAML flow, organizations can dynamically adjust authentication requirements or deny access altogether if certain conditions are met. For example, if a login attempt is detected from an unfamiliar location or a device that hasn't been registered, the IdP can trigger additional verification steps or block the attempt entirely. This technique is particularly valuable for organizations with remote workforces or global operations, as it provides granular control over who can access resources and under what circumstances.

Encryption of specific SAML assertions and attributes is another advanced configuration technique that enhances the confidentiality of sensitive information. While signing assertions ensures data integrity and authenticity, encryption protects the content of the assertions from unauthorized access during transmission. In complex environments, organizations may choose to encrypt only certain attributes within the SAML assertion—such as social security numbers, financial data, or health information—while leaving less sensitive attributes unencrypted for easier processing. This selective encryption approach balances security and performance, ensuring that sensitive data is protected without unnecessarily complicating the processing of non-sensitive information.

Configuring high-availability (HA) and load-balanced SAML environments is crucial for organizations with large-scale or mission-critical applications. In such setups, the IdP and SPs are distributed across multiple servers to ensure redundancy and improve performance. Load balancers distribute authentication requests evenly across available servers, reducing latency and preventing any single server from becoming a bottleneck. Implementing HA configurations requires careful synchronization of metadata, cryptographic keys, and session management across all instances of the IdP and SP. Ensuring that all components are in sync is vital to maintaining a seamless user experience and preventing authentication failures in the event of server outages.

Single Logout (SLO) customization is another area where advanced SAML techniques come into play. While SLO allows users to log out from all federated applications simultaneously, implementing it in complex environments can be challenging due to variations in how different SPs handle logout requests. Advanced SLO configurations involve customizing the logout flow to accommodate these differences, ensuring that all SPs correctly process logout requests and terminate sessions. This may include adjusting binding methods, modifying logout response handling, or implementing custom scripts to manage session termination across diverse applications.

Attribute-based access control (ABAC) is an advanced technique that extends beyond simple role-based access control (RBAC). In ABAC, access decisions are based on a combination of user attributes, environmental conditions, and resource-specific policies. By integrating ABAC into SAML assertions, organizations can implement dynamic access control policies that adapt to various contexts. For instance, access to a particular application might be granted only if the user belongs to a specific department, is accessing from an approved location, and is using a secure device. This granular control enhances security and ensures that access is granted based on a comprehensive evaluation of risk factors.

Integrating SAML with other identity standards like OAuth 2.0 and OpenID Connect (OIDC) is another advanced configuration technique that enhances interoperability across diverse application ecosystems. While SAML excels in enterprise SSO for web-based applications, OAuth and OIDC are better suited for mobile apps and API-based services. By configuring a federation gateway or using an identity provider that supports multiple protocols, organizations can bridge the gap between SAML and these modern standards. This integration allows users to authenticate using SAML credentials while accessing applications that rely on OAuth or OIDC, creating a unified and seamless authentication experience across the entire IT landscape.

Just-In-Time (JIT) provisioning is another advanced feature that streamlines user management in SAML environments. With JIT provisioning, user accounts are automatically created in the service provider's system the first time a user authenticates via SAML. This eliminates the need for manual account creation and ensures that user information is consistently synchronized between the IdP and SP. Advanced JIT provisioning configurations can include attribute mapping rules that determine how user data is structured, as well as conditional logic that controls when and how new accounts are created.

Configuring delegated authentication and impersonation is another complex SAML scenario that requires careful planning and security considerations. Delegated authentication allows one entity to authenticate on behalf of another, while impersonation enables an administrator or support staff to access a user's account for troubleshooting or management purposes. Implementing these features securely involves setting strict policies and controls to prevent abuse, ensuring that only authorized personnel can perform delegated actions, and maintaining detailed audit logs to track all activity.

Advanced logging and monitoring configurations are essential for maintaining the security and integrity of SAML environments. By enabling detailed logging of authentication events, assertion processing, and error handling, organizations can gain deep insights into their identity management systems. Integrating these logs with Security Information and Event Management (SIEM) solutions allows for real-time analysis and alerts, helping detect and respond to suspicious activities or potential security breaches. Advanced monitoring configurations can also include custom dashboards that provide visibility into key metrics, such as authentication success rates, login times, and user access patterns.

Key management and rotation is a crucial aspect of maintaining a secure SAML environment. Regularly rotating cryptographic keys and certificates helps mitigate the risk of key compromise and ensures compliance with security best practices. Advanced key management involves automating the key rotation process, ensuring that all affected metadata is updated and distributed to federated partners without disrupting authentication services. This requires careful coordination and testing to ensure that new keys are correctly recognized and validated across all IdPs and SPs.

Custom error handling and user experience customization are additional advanced techniques that enhance the usability and accessibility of SAML-enabled applications. By customizing error messages and login flows, organizations can provide clearer guidance to users when issues arise, such as failed authentications or session timeouts. Advanced configurations can also include branding and theming options that align the SAML login experience with the organization's visual identity, creating a consistent and professional user interface.

Implementing federation hubs or multi-tenant SAML configurations is another advanced technique that simplifies identity management across large, distributed environments. Federation hubs act as intermediaries between multiple IdPs and SPs, centralizing authentication and trust relationships. This approach is particularly useful in multi-tenant scenarios, such as SaaS applications serving multiple organizations, where each tenant uses its own IdP for authentication. Advanced configurations allow for flexible policy management, tenant-specific attribute mappings, and scalable infrastructure to support a growing number of federated partners.

By mastering these advanced SAML configuration techniques, organizations can build robust, secure, and flexible identity management systems that meet the demands of complex IT environments. Whether enhancing security with multi-factor authentication, integrating with modern identity standards, or implementing dynamic access controls, these techniques provide the tools needed to optimize and future-proof SAML deployments.

Chapter 24: Using SAML with Mobile Applications

As mobile applications become increasingly central to how users access services and perform tasks, securing authentication processes for these applications is more critical than ever. Security Assertion Markup Language (SAML) has long been a standard for providing Single Sign-On (SSO) and federated identity management in web applications, but extending SAML's capabilities to mobile platforms introduces unique challenges and opportunities. While SAML was originally designed with web browsers in mind, with proper configuration and the right tools, it can effectively secure mobile applications and provide a seamless authentication experience for users on the go.

The primary challenge of using SAML with mobile applications lies in its reliance on browser-based redirection flows. Traditional SAML authentication involves redirecting the user from a Service Provider (SP) to an Identity Provider (IdP) in a web browser, where the user logs in and is then redirected back to the SP with a SAML assertion. This flow works well for desktop environments where browsers are the primary interface, but mobile applications typically operate within their own native environments, making it less straightforward to handle browser redirects.

One common solution to this challenge is the use of embedded web views within mobile applications. A web view is a browser-like component that can be embedded in a mobile app to load web content, including authentication pages. When integrating SAML with a mobile app, the app can launch a web view to handle the SAML authentication process, redirecting the user to the IdP's login page within the app and capturing the SAML assertion upon successful authentication. This approach allows developers to leverage existing SAML infrastructure while providing a seamless experience that keeps users within the app environment.

However, using web views for SAML authentication comes with security considerations. Web views may not offer the same level of security as external browsers, particularly when it comes to protecting user credentials from malicious interception. To mitigate these risks, many security experts recommend using external browser-based SSO flows instead of embedded web views. In this model, the mobile app launches the device's default browser to handle the SAML authentication process. Once the user authenticates in the browser, the app captures the SAML assertion through a registered callback or deep link. This method leverages the security features of modern browsers, such as secure cookie handling and sandboxing, while maintaining the SSO experience.

Implementing SAML in mobile applications also requires careful handling of session management. Unlike web applications, which rely on browser cookies to maintain sessions, mobile apps must manage sessions within the app itself. After receiving a SAML assertion, the app typically exchanges it for a session token or access token, which is then stored securely on the device, often in an encrypted storage area like the Keychain on iOS or Keystore on Android. Proper token management is essential to ensure that sessions are securely maintained and that tokens are invalidated when the user logs out or when they expire.

To simplify the process of integrating SAML with mobile applications, many developers turn to third-party libraries and SDKs that abstract the complexities of SAML authentication. Libraries such as AppAuth or platform-specific SDKs provided by identity providers (like Okta or Azure AD) offer pre-built functions to handle the SAML flow, manage tokens, and interact with authentication endpoints. These tools streamline the development process and ensure that security best practices are followed, reducing the likelihood of introducing vulnerabilities during implementation.

Another approach to using SAML in mobile applications involves leveraging identity brokers or federation gateways. These intermediaries translate SAML assertions into more mobile-friendly protocols like OAuth 2.0 or OpenID Connect (OIDC). While SAML remains the backbone for federated identity in many enterprise environments, OAuth and OIDC are better suited for mobile and API-based authentication due to their lightweight JSON format and token-based architecture. By integrating a federation gateway, organizations can authenticate users through SAML while providing mobile apps with OAuth tokens, combining the strengths of both protocols and enhancing the overall user experience.

Security remains a paramount concern when using SAML with mobile applications. Transport Layer Security (TLS) must be enforced for all communications between the mobile app, the IdP, and any intermediary services to protect against man-in-the-middle attacks. Additionally, mobile apps must validate the SAML assertions they receive to ensure they originate from a trusted IdP and have not been tampered with during transmission. This involves verifying digital signatures and checking the assertion's validity conditions, such as timestamps and audience restrictions.

Single Logout (SLO) is another feature that can be implemented in mobile applications to enhance security. SLO ensures that when a user logs out from one application, their sessions are terminated across all connected apps and services. Implementing SLO in mobile apps requires careful coordination between the app, the IdP, and any other service providers in the federation. The app must be able to handle logout requests from the IdP and ensure that any stored tokens are securely deleted from the device.

For organizations with bring-your-own-device (BYOD) policies, using SAML in mobile applications adds an additional layer of security and control. SAML allows organizations to enforce consistent authentication policies across all devices, regardless of whether they are corporate-issued or personal. By integrating SAML with mobile device management (MDM) solutions, organizations can further secure mobile access, applying conditional access policies based on device compliance, encryption status, or the presence of security features like biometric authentication.

In enterprise environments, SAML is often used to provide seamless access to corporate resources through mobile applications. For example, employees might use a mobile app to access internal systems like intranets, HR portals, or project management tools. By integrating SAML, these apps can authenticate users against the organization's central identity provider, ensuring that the same security policies applied to desktop access are enforced on mobile devices. This unified approach simplifies user management and enhances security by reducing the number of disparate authentication systems that need to be maintained.

Healthcare and financial services are two industries where using SAML with mobile applications is particularly valuable. In healthcare, mobile apps often provide access to sensitive patient information, making secure authentication essential to comply with regulations like HIPAA. SAML enables healthcare providers to authenticate mobile users through their existing identity infrastructure, ensuring that patient data is accessed securely and only by authorized personnel. Similarly, in financial services, mobile apps that allow users to access account information or perform transactions must adhere to stringent security standards. SAML integration helps ensure that these apps meet regulatory requirements like PCI DSS while providing a seamless user experience.

Educational institutions also benefit from integrating SAML with mobile applications. Students, faculty, and staff often access learning management systems (LMS), library resources, and collaboration tools through mobile apps. By leveraging SAML, educational institutions can provide SSO across all these resources, allowing users to authenticate once with their campus credentials and gain access to a wide range of services. This simplifies access for users while reducing the administrative burden of managing multiple accounts.

While integrating SAML with mobile applications offers numerous benefits, it is not without challenges. The complexity of handling browser redirects, managing sessions, and securing tokens requires careful planning and implementation. Additionally, the diverse nature of mobile platforms and devices means that testing and compatibility checks are essential to ensure a consistent and secure user experience across all environments.

Despite these challenges, the flexibility and security provided by SAML make it a valuable tool for mobile application authentication. By leveraging existing identity infrastructure, organizations can provide a seamless and secure authentication experience for mobile users, whether they are employees accessing internal systems, customers engaging with a service, or students using educational resources. With the right tools and best practices, SAML can be effectively integrated into mobile applications, supporting the growing demand for secure, convenient access to services on the go.

Chapter 25: Performance Optimization in SAML Implementations

As organizations increasingly rely on Security Assertion Markup Language (SAML) for federated identity management and Single Sign-On (SSO) solutions, ensuring optimal performance becomes critical. While SAML provides robust security and seamless user authentication across multiple services, its XML-based structure and complex message exchanges can introduce latency and processing overhead if not properly managed. Performance optimization in SAML implementations is essential to maintain a smooth user experience, particularly in high-traffic environments or large-scale enterprises. This chapter explores various strategies to enhance the efficiency, responsiveness, and scalability of SAML-based systems.

A key factor affecting SAML performance is the processing of XML-based SAML assertions. Unlike lightweight protocols such as OAuth 2.0, which use JSON for data representation, SAML relies on verbose XML documents. Parsing and validating these XML messages can be resource-intensive, especially when digital signatures and encryption are involved. To mitigate this overhead, organizations can optimize their XML parsing mechanisms. Using streaming XML parsers like SAX (Simple API for XML) instead of DOM (Document Object Model) parsers reduces memory consumption and speeds up processing, as SAX parsers read XML data sequentially without loading the entire document into memory.

Another critical performance consideration is the management of cryptographic operations. SAML assertions are typically signed and sometimes encrypted to ensure integrity and confidentiality. While these security measures are essential, they can also slow down authentication if not efficiently handled. To optimize cryptographic performance, organizations should use hardware security modules

(HSMs) or dedicated cryptographic accelerators to offload the processing of digital signatures and encryption tasks. Additionally, selecting modern, efficient cryptographic algorithms like ECDSA over traditional RSA can significantly improve signing and verification speeds without compromising security.

Session management is another area where performance optimization can yield substantial benefits. In SAML-based SSO environments, maintaining user sessions efficiently is crucial for minimizing authentication latency. Instead of re-authenticating users for every service access, organizations can implement session caching mechanisms that store validated SAML assertions or session tokens. This reduces redundant processing and speeds up subsequent logins. Properly configured session timeouts and revalidation intervals ensure that sessions remain secure while optimizing performance.

The size of SAML assertions also impacts performance. Large assertions containing numerous attributes can increase processing time and network latency. To address this, organizations should adopt attribute minimization strategies, including only the essential attributes required by the service provider in the SAML assertion. By reducing the payload size, the time needed for parsing, transmitting, and validating assertions decreases, leading to faster authentication processes.

Another optimization technique involves metadata management. SAML relies heavily on metadata exchanges between identity providers (IdPs) and service providers (SPs) to establish trust relationships and configure communication endpoints. In large federations with numerous entities, metadata files can become extensive, affecting performance during metadata parsing and validation. To optimize this, organizations should periodically prune and clean metadata, removing outdated or unnecessary entries. Additionally, leveraging metadata caching at both the IdP and SP levels minimizes the need for repeated metadata processing, improving overall system responsiveness.

Network latency plays a significant role in SAML performance, particularly in distributed environments where IdPs and SPs are geographically dispersed. Implementing content delivery networks (CDNs) and edge caching for static resources like metadata files can reduce the time required to retrieve necessary information during authentication. Moreover, optimizing DNS resolution by using low-latency DNS servers and ensuring that IdP and SP endpoints are accessible via high-speed, low-latency network paths can further enhance performance.

Load balancing and high availability configurations are essential for scaling SAML implementations in high-traffic environments. Deploying multiple instances of IdPs and SPs behind load balancers distributes authentication requests evenly across available resources, preventing any single server from becoming a bottleneck. Load balancers can also provide health checks to ensure that only healthy servers handle requests, enhancing reliability and uptime. Additionally, implementing failover mechanisms ensures that if one IdP or SP instance fails, another can seamlessly take over, maintaining uninterrupted authentication services.

Asynchronous processing is another advanced technique to optimize SAML performance. In scenarios where SAML assertions trigger additional processing, such as fetching user attributes from external directories or logging detailed audit information, asynchronous handling can prevent delays in the authentication flow. By decoupling these tasks from the main authentication process and handling them in the background, organizations can reduce latency and improve the overall user experience.

Optimizing the binding methods used in SAML communications also contributes to performance improvements. SAML supports various bindings, such as HTTP Redirect, HTTP POST, and Artifact binding. While HTTP POST is commonly used for transmitting assertions due to its support for larger payloads, it can introduce latency due to the need for server-side form processing. In contrast, HTTP Redirect binding is faster for smaller messages but limited by URL length constraints. Artifact binding offers a hybrid approach, transmitting a lightweight artifact via HTTP Redirect and retrieving the full assertion via a back-channel SOAP request. Selecting the most appropriate binding based on message size, network conditions, and security requirements can optimize performance.

Database performance tuning is crucial when SAML implementations rely on backend databases for storing session information, user attributes, or audit logs. Optimizing database queries, indexing relevant fields, and using connection pooling techniques can significantly reduce database-related latency during authentication processes. Additionally, implementing in-memory data stores like Redis or Memcached for session management and attribute caching can further enhance performance by reducing reliance on slower disk-based databases.

Monitoring and analytics play a vital role in identifying performance bottlenecks and optimizing SAML implementations. By deploying performance monitoring tools that track key metrics such as authentication response times, server load, and network latency, organizations can gain insights into the system's performance. Regularly analyzing these metrics helps identify areas for improvement, such as optimizing server configurations, adjusting timeout settings, or scaling infrastructure to meet increasing demand.

Optimizing logging practices also contributes to better performance in SAML environments. While logging is essential for auditing and troubleshooting, excessive or verbose logging can slow down authentication processes, especially in high-traffic systems. Configuring log levels appropriately—enabling detailed logs only when necessary and focusing on critical events—ensures that logging does not become a performance bottleneck. Additionally, using log rotation and archiving strategies prevents log files from growing too large, which can degrade system performance.

Client-side optimizations can further enhance the user experience in SAML-based systems. Reducing the time it takes for browsers to process SAML responses involves optimizing JavaScript execution, minimizing the use of large, complex forms for SAML POST responses, and ensuring that browser caches are leveraged effectively. For mobile applications, optimizing how SAML assertions are handled within embedded web views or external browsers ensures that the authentication process is swift and seamless.

Implementing compression techniques for SAML messages can reduce the size of transmitted data, improving network performance.

Protocols like GZIP can be enabled on web servers to compress SAML assertions and metadata during transmission, reducing bandwidth usage and speeding up data transfer. This is particularly beneficial in environments with limited network resources or when transmitting large amounts of metadata between federated partners.

Security configurations can also impact performance, and striking the right balance between security and efficiency is essential. While strong encryption and comprehensive signature validation are critical for protecting SAML assertions, using overly complex cryptographic algorithms or excessively long key lengths can introduce unnecessary latency. Organizations should adhere to industry-standard security practices, using recommended key lengths and algorithms that provide robust security without compromising performance.

Finally, periodic performance reviews and updates are essential to maintaining an optimized SAML environment. As technology evolves and user demands increase, regular assessments of the SAML infrastructure ensure that it continues to meet performance expectations. Updating software components, applying performance patches, and staying informed about best practices in SAML implementations help organizations maintain a secure, efficient, and scalable identity management system.

By applying these performance optimization techniques, organizations can ensure that their SAML implementations provide fast, reliable, and secure authentication services, meeting the demands of modern enterprise environments while delivering an excellent user experience.

Chapter 26: Best Practices for SAML Security

Security Assertion Markup Language (SAML) has become a cornerstone of federated identity management and Single Sign-On (SSO) solutions, enabling secure authentication and authorization across diverse applications and organizations. While SAML provides a robust framework for exchanging authentication information, its effectiveness relies heavily on proper configuration and the implementation of security best practices. Misconfigurations or oversights can expose organizations to significant risks, including unauthorized access, data breaches, and impersonation attacks. To ensure the integrity, confidentiality, and reliability of SAML-based systems, organizations must adopt a comprehensive set of security practices.

A foundational best practice in SAML security is the use of digital signatures on all SAML assertions. Digital signatures ensure the integrity and authenticity of the assertion, allowing the Service Provider (SP) to verify that the assertion was issued by a trusted Identity Provider (IdP) and has not been altered in transit. The IdP should sign every assertion using a secure private key, and the SP must rigorously validate the signature using the corresponding public key provided in the IdP's metadata. Ensuring that both parties correctly implement signature verification is critical to preventing assertion forgery and man-in-the-middle (MITM) attacks.

In addition to signing, encryption plays a vital role in protecting the confidentiality of sensitive data transmitted in SAML assertions. While signatures prevent tampering, encryption ensures that only the intended recipient can access the data. Organizations should encrypt assertions or specific attributes within assertions, especially when they contain sensitive information such as user roles, personal identifiers, or session tokens. The SP's public key, included in its metadata, is used by the IdP to encrypt the data, while the SP's private key is used to decrypt it. This dual use of signing and encryption creates a layered defense that protects both the integrity and confidentiality of SAML messages.

Another critical security best practice is ensuring secure transport of SAML messages. All communications between the user's browser, the IdP, and the SP should be transmitted over Transport Layer Security (TLS) to protect against interception and eavesdropping. TLS not only encrypts the data in transit but also provides endpoint authentication, ensuring that messages are sent to and received from legitimate servers. Organizations should enforce the use of HTTPS for all SAML-related endpoints and configure their servers to use strong, up-to-date TLS protocols and ciphers.

Strict validation of SAML assertions is essential to preventing unauthorized access. When an SP receives a SAML assertion, it must validate several key elements beyond the digital signature. These include the Issuer field, which identifies the IdP; the AudienceRestriction condition, which specifies the intended recipient of the assertion; and the validity period of the assertion, defined by the NotBefore and NotOnOrAfter timestamps. Failing to enforce these checks can leave systems vulnerable to replay attacks or assertion misuse by malicious actors.

To mitigate the risk of replay attacks, organizations should implement mechanisms to detect and reject previously used assertions. SAML assertions often include a unique SessionIndex or Assertion ID that can be tracked by the SP to ensure that each assertion is used only once. Additionally, assertions should have short validity periods, limiting the window of opportunity for attackers to capture and reuse them. Configuring SPs to reject assertions that fall outside the specified validity period is a simple yet effective way to enhance security.

Metadata management is another cornerstone of SAML security. Metadata contains critical information about the IdP and SP, including their endpoints, supported bindings, and cryptographic keys. Ensuring that metadata is accurate, up-to-date, and securely distributed is essential for maintaining trust relationships between entities. Metadata should be signed to verify its authenticity, and any changes—such as key rotations or endpoint updates—should be promptly communicated and applied to all federated partners. Regularly reviewing and auditing metadata helps prevent configuration drift and reduces the risk of security vulnerabilities.

Key management is a fundamental aspect of securing SAML environments. Both the IdP and SP rely on cryptographic keys for signing and encrypting SAML messages. These keys must be generated using strong algorithms, stored securely, and protected from unauthorized access. Organizations should implement robust key management practices, including hardware security modules (HSMs) for secure key storage, regular key rotations to mitigate the risk of key compromise, and revocation mechanisms to invalidate keys that are no longer secure. When rotating keys, it is crucial to update metadata accordingly and ensure that all federated partners are aware of the changes.

Implementing multi-factor authentication (MFA) at the IdP level significantly enhances the security of SAML-based systems. MFA requires users to provide additional verification, such as a one-time password (OTP) or biometric factor, beyond their primary credentials. This added layer of security protects against credential theft and phishing attacks, ensuring that even if a user's password is compromised, unauthorized access is still prevented. Integrating MFA into the SAML authentication flow provides consistent, robust security across all federated applications and services.

Organizations should also adopt principle of least privilege when configuring SAML attribute release policies. Only the minimum necessary attributes should be included in SAML assertions to reduce the risk of sensitive information exposure. For example, if an SP only requires a user's email address for authentication, additional attributes such as roles, departments, or personal identifiers should not be included. Carefully defining and auditing attribute release policies ensures that user data is shared appropriately and securely.

Session management practices are critical to maintaining secure SAML implementations. After a user is authenticated via SAML, the SP typically establishes a session that allows continued access without re-authentication. Organizations should implement secure session handling practices, including session timeouts, automatic session termination after periods of inactivity, and session invalidation upon logout. Additionally, implementing Single Logout (SLO) ensures that when a user logs out from one federated application, all active sessions across the federation are terminated, reducing the risk of session hijacking.

Monitoring and auditing are essential components of a secure SAML environment. Organizations should log all SAML-related events, including authentication requests, assertion processing, and logout activities. These logs provide valuable insights into user activity, help detect suspicious behavior, and support forensic investigations in the event of a security incident. Integrating SAML logs with Security Information and Event Management (SIEM) systems allows for real-time monitoring, automated threat detection, and centralized incident response.

Error handling in SAML implementations should be carefully managed to avoid exposing sensitive information. Detailed error messages can provide attackers with valuable clues about system configurations, vulnerabilities, or potential attack vectors. Organizations should ensure that error messages are generic and do not reveal internal details, while detailed logs are maintained securely for administrative review. Additionally, using custom error pages can provide users with clear guidance without disclosing sensitive information.

In federated environments involving multiple organizations, establishing clear trust and governance policies is essential. Organizations should define and document the processes for onboarding new federated partners, managing metadata exchanges, and handling security incidents. Regular security assessments and compliance audits help ensure that all federated entities adhere to agreed-upon security standards and best practices.

Regular security updates and patches are crucial for maintaining a secure SAML environment. SAML software, libraries, and supporting infrastructure should be kept up-to-date with the latest security patches and updates. Vulnerabilities in SAML implementations can be exploited by attackers if not promptly addressed, so organizations must monitor for security advisories and apply updates in a timely manner. Additionally, vulnerability scanning and penetration testing can help identify potential weaknesses in the SAML system before they can be exploited.

Education and training play a vital role in maintaining SAML security. Administrators and developers responsible for configuring and managing SAML implementations should receive ongoing training on best practices, security standards, and emerging threats. Users should also be educated about safe authentication practices, recognizing phishing attempts, and the importance of secure password management.

By adopting these best practices, organizations can build and maintain secure, resilient SAML implementations that protect user identities, safeguard sensitive data, and provide reliable authentication services across diverse applications and environments. As the threat landscape continues to evolve, staying informed and proactive in applying security measures is essential to ensuring the long-term security and integrity of SAML-based systems.

Chapter 27: Testing and Debugging SAML Integrations

Implementing Security Assertion Markup Language (SAML) in an organization's authentication infrastructure offers a powerful means to achieve Single Sign-On (SSO) and federated identity management. However, due to the complexity of SAML protocols, debugging and testing integrations can often be challenging. A successful SAML deployment requires meticulous testing at each stage, from initial configuration to full-scale production, to ensure that the identity provider (IdP) and service provider (SP) communicate effectively and securely.

The first step in testing a SAML integration is verifying that the metadata exchange between the IdP and SP is correctly configured. Metadata is the backbone of a SAML configuration, containing crucial information about endpoints, supported bindings, and cryptographic keys. An incorrect or outdated metadata file can lead to failed authentications or broken communication channels. During testing, administrators should ensure that both the IdP and SP are using the most recent metadata files and that the entity IDs, SSO URLs, and certificate fingerprints match between systems. Any discrepancies in the metadata can result in the SP rejecting assertions or the IdP failing to process authentication requests.

One of the most common issues encountered in SAML integrations involves digital signature validation. SAML assertions are typically signed by the IdP to ensure authenticity and integrity. If the SP cannot validate the signature, it will reject the assertion, preventing successful authentication. When testing, administrators should verify that the IdP's public key is correctly imported into the SP's configuration. They should also check that the signing algorithm used by the IdP is supported by the SP. A mismatch in cryptographic algorithms or an expired certificate can cause signature validation to fail. Reviewing SAML logs and error messages can help pinpoint these issues, as they often contain detailed information about the specific cause of the failure.

Another critical aspect of testing SAML integrations is ensuring that time synchronization between the IdP and SP is accurate. SAML assertions include time-sensitive conditions, such as NotBefore and NotOnOrAfter timestamps, which define the validity window of the assertion. If the clocks on the IdP and SP servers are out of sync, assertions may appear expired or not yet valid, leading to authentication failures. To prevent this, both systems should be configured to synchronize with a reliable Network Time Protocol (NTP) server. Testing should include verifying that the timestamps in the assertions align with the expected timeframes on both the IdP and SP sides.

Testing the SAML binding methods used for communication is also essential. SAML supports various bindings, such as HTTP Redirect, HTTP POST, and HTTP Artifact. Each binding method has its specific implementation requirements and potential pitfalls. For example, HTTP Redirect binding is suitable for lightweight messages but can run into URL length limitations, while HTTP POST binding is better for transmitting larger assertions but may encounter issues with browser compatibility or form submissions. During testing, administrators should verify that the chosen binding methods are correctly configured and supported by both the IdP and SP. They should also test fallback mechanisms to ensure that alternative bindings function as expected if the primary method fails.

Attribute mapping and transformation is another area that often requires careful testing. The IdP sends user attributes in the SAML assertion, such as email, username, or group memberships, which the SP uses to provision access and define user roles. If the SP does not receive the expected attributes or if they are incorrectly formatted, users may experience access issues or receive inappropriate permissions. Testing should include verifying that the IdP is sending the correct attributes, that the attribute names and formats match the SP's expectations, and that any attribute transformations are applied correctly. Tools like SAML tracers and browser developer consoles can help capture and inspect the SAML assertions to ensure that attributes are correctly passed and interpreted.

Testing should also cover error handling and user feedback. When authentication fails, users should receive clear, actionable error messages that guide them on how to resolve the issue, without exposing sensitive system details. During testing, administrators should simulate various failure scenarios, such as incorrect credentials, expired certificates, or invalid assertions, to verify that the system handles errors gracefully and provides appropriate feedback to users. This not only enhances the user experience but also helps identify potential weaknesses in the system's error-handling mechanisms.

Single Logout (SLO) functionality should be tested to ensure that sessions are properly terminated across all federated applications. SLO allows users to log out from one application and have their sessions automatically closed on all other connected applications. Testing SLO involves verifying that logout requests are correctly propagated from the SP to the IdP and then to other SPs, and that each entity properly handles the logout process. Administrators should also test scenarios where one or more SPs fail to respond to logout requests, ensuring that the system can handle partial logouts without leaving sessions active.

Another important aspect of testing SAML integrations is ensuring security and compliance. This includes verifying that all assertions are signed and, if necessary, encrypted, and that secure protocols like TLS are used for all communications. Security testing should also involve checking for common vulnerabilities, such as XML Signature Wrapping (XSW) attacks, which exploit weaknesses in how XML signatures are validated. Administrators should use security testing tools to scan for potential vulnerabilities and ensure that the system adheres to best practices for secure SAML implementation.

To streamline the testing and debugging process, organizations can use automated testing tools that simulate SAML authentication flows and validate the responses. Tools like SAMLtest, SSOCheck, and various open-source SAML libraries provide automated ways to test different aspects of the SAML integration, from metadata validation to assertion processing. These tools can quickly identify configuration errors, missing attributes, or signature validation issues, allowing administrators to address problems before they affect end users.

Monitoring and logging are essential for ongoing debugging and performance optimization. Detailed logs should be enabled on both the IdP and SP to capture authentication requests, assertion processing, and error messages. These logs provide valuable insights into the system's behavior and can help identify the root cause of issues when they arise. Integrating SAML logs with a Security Information and Event Management (SIEM) system allows for real-time monitoring, alerting, and analysis of authentication events, helping to detect and respond to security incidents more effectively.

Finally, collaboration between teams is crucial for successful SAML integration testing. SAML often involves multiple stakeholders, including identity administrators, application developers, and security teams. Effective communication and coordination between these groups ensure that configurations are aligned, issues are quickly identified and resolved, and the overall integration process runs smoothly. Regular meetings, shared documentation, and clear escalation paths help foster a collaborative environment that supports successful SAML deployments.

By following these best practices for testing and debugging SAML integrations, organizations can ensure that their identity management systems are secure, reliable, and efficient. Thorough testing at each stage of the integration process, combined with effective monitoring and collaboration, helps prevent common pitfalls and delivers a seamless authentication experience for users across federated applications and services.

Chapter 28: Identity Federation Across Organizations

In today's interconnected world, collaboration between organizations is more essential than ever. Whether it's businesses partnering on joint ventures, educational institutions sharing research platforms, or government agencies coordinating services, seamless and secure access to shared resources is critical. Identity federation, particularly through protocols like SAML (Security Assertion Markup Language), plays a pivotal role in enabling this secure access by allowing users from different organizations to authenticate using their existing credentials while accessing external systems. This chapter explores how identity federation works across organizations, its benefits, challenges, and best practices for implementation.

Identity federation is the process of linking a user's digital identity across multiple systems and organizations. Instead of maintaining separate credentials for each service or partner organization, users authenticate through their home organization's Identity Provider (IdP), which issues SAML assertions that are trusted by external Service Providers (SPs). This model not only simplifies the user experience by enabling Single Sign-On (SSO) but also enhances security by centralizing authentication and reducing the proliferation of passwords.

At the core of identity federation is the trust relationship between the IdP and SP. This trust is established through the exchange of metadata—XML files containing information about endpoints, supported protocols, and cryptographic keys. Each organization's IdP and SP must be properly configured to recognize and trust each other's metadata, ensuring that authentication requests and responses are securely processed. The use of digital signatures on SAML assertions guarantees the authenticity and integrity of the messages, while encryption protects sensitive user attributes during transmission.

One of the most common scenarios for identity federation across organizations is business-to-business (B2B) collaboration. In these environments, companies need to grant partners, suppliers, or contractors access to specific resources without creating separate accounts in their systems. By federating identities, a company can allow external users to authenticate using their own corporate credentials. This approach reduces administrative overhead, as the partner organization retains responsibility for managing its users' credentials and access policies. It also enhances security by ensuring that only authenticated, authorized users can access shared resources.

In the education sector, identity federation is widely used to facilitate access to academic resources across institutions. Federations like InCommon in the United States and eduGAIN in Europe link universities, research institutions, and service providers in a shared trust framework. Students, faculty, and researchers can use their institutional credentials to access digital libraries, research databases, and collaboration tools hosted by other organizations within the federation. This seamless access promotes academic collaboration and resource sharing while maintaining the security and privacy of user data.

Government agencies also benefit from identity federation when coordinating services across different departments or jurisdictions. For example, a federal agency might need to grant access to its systems to state or local government employees. By establishing federated trust relationships, these employees can use their existing credentials from their home agencies to authenticate securely. This model supports efficient inter-agency collaboration, reduces the administrative burden of managing multiple user accounts, and ensures that sensitive government data is protected through standardized security protocols.

While the benefits of identity federation are significant, implementing it across organizations presents several challenges. One of the primary obstacles is ensuring interoperability between different systems and identity providers. Even though SAML is a standardized protocol, variations in implementation can lead to compatibility issues. Organizations must carefully coordinate their configurations, ensuring that metadata is accurately exchanged and that supported bindings, encryption algorithms, and attribute formats are compatible.

Another challenge is managing attribute mapping and release policies. Different organizations may use varying naming conventions and formats for user attributes, such as roles, departments, or unique identifiers. Service providers need to map incoming attributes to their internal schemas correctly, while identity providers must define clear policies on which attributes to release to external partners. This process requires careful planning and collaboration between organizations to ensure that the necessary information is shared securely and accurately without exposing unnecessary data.

Trust management is at the heart of identity federation, and maintaining trust relationships requires continuous effort. Organizations must regularly update and audit their metadata to reflect changes in endpoints, cryptographic keys, or configurations. They must also establish clear procedures for handling security incidents, such as key compromises or unauthorized access attempts. When a breach occurs in one federated partner, it can potentially impact the entire trust network, so timely communication and coordinated responses are essential to mitigating risks.

Scalability is another important consideration in federated environments. As organizations grow and add more partners to their federations, the complexity of managing trust relationships increases. Federation hubs or identity brokers can simplify this process by acting as intermediaries between multiple IdPs and SPs. Instead of establishing direct trust relationships with each partner, organizations can trust the federation hub, which handles the authentication flow and enforces security policies across the network. This model reduces administrative overhead and simplifies the management of large, complex federations.

Security is a paramount concern in identity federation. Organizations must implement robust security measures to protect SAML assertions and authentication flows. This includes using strong cryptographic algorithms for signing and encrypting assertions, enforcing Transport Layer Security (TLS) for all communications, and validating the integrity of SAML messages. Additionally, federated systems should implement multi-factor authentication (MFA) at the IdP level to enhance security and reduce the risk of credential theft or unauthorized access.

Auditing and monitoring are essential for maintaining the security and integrity of federated identity systems. Organizations should log all authentication events, including successful and failed login attempts, assertion processing, and attribute release activities. These logs provide valuable insights into user behavior and can help detect suspicious activities or potential security breaches. Integrating these logs with Security Information and Event Management (SIEM) solutions enables real-time monitoring and automated threat detection, supporting a proactive security posture.

Governance frameworks play a critical role in the success of federated identity systems. Clear policies and agreements between federated partners define how identities are managed, how data is shared, and how security incidents are handled. These frameworks should address key aspects such as metadata management, attribute release policies, incident response procedures, and compliance with regulatory requirements. Establishing strong governance practices ensures that all federated entities adhere to consistent security standards and operational protocols.

Regulatory compliance is another important consideration in identity federation, particularly in industries subject to strict data protection and privacy regulations. Protocols like SAML support compliance with regulations such as the General Data Protection Regulation (GDPR) in the European Union, the Health Insurance Portability and Accountability Act (HIPAA) in the healthcare sector, and the Federal Risk and Authorization Management Program (FedRAMP) in the United States. By enforcing secure authentication practices, protecting user data, and maintaining detailed audit logs, federated identity systems can meet regulatory requirements while enabling efficient collaboration across organizations.

The rise of cloud computing has further expanded the role of identity federation in modern IT environments. Many organizations use cloud-based applications and services that require secure, federated authentication. SAML provides a standardized way to integrate on-premises identity systems with cloud platforms like Microsoft 365, Google Workspace, AWS, and Salesforce. By federating identities across on-premises and cloud environments, organizations can provide a seamless user experience while maintaining centralized control over authentication and access policies.

Cross-border collaborations introduce additional complexities in identity federation, particularly when different legal and regulatory frameworks come into play. Organizations participating in international federations must navigate varying data protection laws, privacy standards, and compliance requirements. Establishing clear agreements and aligning security practices across jurisdictions is essential to ensuring that federated identity systems operate smoothly and securely on a global scale.

Despite the challenges, identity federation across organizations offers immense benefits in terms of security, efficiency, and user experience. By enabling secure, seamless access to shared resources, federated identity systems support collaboration, innovation, and operational agility. Through careful planning, robust security practices, and strong governance frameworks, organizations can build and maintain effective federated identity systems that meet the demands of today's interconnected world.

Chapter 29: Handling SAML in Hybrid Environments

As organizations increasingly adopt hybrid IT environments, combining on-premises infrastructure with cloud-based services, managing authentication and identity securely across these diverse ecosystems becomes a critical challenge. Security Assertion Markup Language (SAML) serves as a vital protocol in addressing these challenges, providing a standardized framework for Single Sign-On (SSO) and federated identity management. Successfully handling SAML in hybrid environments requires a nuanced understanding of both the technical and strategic considerations involved in bridging disparate systems while maintaining security, performance, and user experience.

In a hybrid environment, organizations often maintain legacy on-premises applications and systems alongside modern cloud services such as Microsoft 365, Google Workspace, and AWS. SAML facilitates seamless authentication across these platforms by enabling users to authenticate once with a central Identity Provider (IdP) and gain access to multiple services, whether hosted on-premises or in the cloud. This unified authentication approach not only enhances security by centralizing credential management but also improves user experience by reducing the need for multiple logins.

One of the primary considerations when implementing SAML in hybrid environments is the integration of on-premises IdPs with cloud-based Service Providers (SPs). Organizations typically use existing directory services like Active Directory (AD) or Lightweight Directory Access Protocol (LDAP) to manage user identities on-premises. To extend these identities to the cloud, SAML-based IdPs such as Active Directory Federation Services (ADFS) or Azure Active Directory (Azure AD) are commonly deployed. These IdPs act as intermediaries, authenticating users against the on-premises directory and issuing SAML assertions that allow access to cloud applications.

Setting up this integration involves configuring federation trust relationships between the IdP and each cloud SP. This is achieved by exchanging metadata files that contain information about endpoints, supported bindings, and cryptographic keys. Proper metadata management is crucial in hybrid environments, as it ensures that all entities recognize and trust each other. Administrators must ensure that metadata is regularly updated and securely distributed to reflect changes such as key rotations, endpoint modifications, or new service integrations.

Another key aspect of handling SAML in hybrid environments is ensuring secure and reliable connectivity between on-premises systems and cloud services. This often requires setting up secure communication channels, such as Virtual Private Networks (VPNs) or dedicated network links, to ensure that SAML assertions and authentication requests are transmitted securely. Additionally, organizations should enforce Transport Layer Security (TLS) for all SAML communications to protect against interception and tampering.

High availability and failover configurations are essential in hybrid environments to ensure continuous authentication services. On-premises IdPs must be configured for redundancy, with load balancers distributing authentication requests across multiple servers to prevent any single point of failure. In the event of an outage in the on-premises infrastructure, failover mechanisms should be in place to redirect authentication requests to backup IdPs or cloud-based identity services. This ensures that users retain access to critical applications even during infrastructure disruptions.

Managing identity synchronization between on-premises directories and cloud services is another critical consideration. While SAML facilitates federated authentication, it does not inherently handle identity provisioning or synchronization. Tools like Azure AD Connect or third-party identity management solutions can synchronize user accounts, groups, and attributes from on-premises directories to cloud-based identity platforms. This synchronization ensures that user information is consistent across environments, enabling seamless SSO and accurate access control.

Attribute mapping and transformation play a significant role in ensuring that user attributes from on-premises directories are correctly interpreted by cloud services. Different applications may require specific attributes or formats, necessitating the transformation of attributes within the SAML assertion. For example, an on-premises directory might store a user's role as "Manager," while a cloud application expects the attribute to be "admin." Configuring the IdP to map and transform attributes accordingly ensures that users receive appropriate access and permissions across all integrated services.

Security remains a paramount concern when handling SAML in hybrid environments. Organizations must implement robust key management practices, including regular rotation of cryptographic keys used for signing and encrypting SAML assertions. Both the IdP and SP must be configured to trust the correct keys, and metadata should be updated promptly to reflect any changes. Additionally, implementing multi-factor authentication (MFA) at the IdP level enhances security by requiring additional verification steps for users accessing sensitive applications, whether on-premises or in the cloud.

Session management in hybrid environments presents unique challenges, as users may have active sessions across both on-premises and cloud applications. Implementing Single Logout (SLO) ensures that when a user logs out from one service, their sessions are terminated across all connected applications. This requires careful coordination between the IdP and SPs to propagate logout requests and handle session termination correctly. Proper session timeout configurations and periodic re-authentication requirements further enhance security by minimizing the risk of session hijacking.

Monitoring and auditing are essential for maintaining the security and performance of SAML integrations in hybrid environments. Detailed logs of authentication events, assertion processing, and error messages should be collected from both on-premises and cloud systems. These logs provide valuable insights into user activity, help detect suspicious behavior, and support compliance with regulatory requirements. Integrating SAML logs with Security Information and Event Management (SIEM) solutions enables centralized monitoring and real-time threat detection across the hybrid environment.

Performance optimization is another critical factor in handling SAML in hybrid environments. The XML-based nature of SAML assertions and the complexity of cryptographic operations can introduce latency, particularly when authentication requests must traverse network boundaries between on-premises and cloud systems. To optimize performance, organizations can implement caching mechanisms for session tokens and metadata, reducing redundant processing and network overhead. Additionally, optimizing network paths and minimizing latency between the IdP and SPs ensures faster authentication responses and a smoother user experience.

As hybrid environments evolve, organizations must also consider scalability when designing their SAML architecture. As the number of integrated applications and users grows, the IdP must be capable of handling increased authentication traffic without performance degradation. This may involve scaling the IdP infrastructure horizontally by adding more servers or leveraging cloud-based identity services that can automatically scale to meet demand. Ensuring that the SAML configuration is flexible and adaptable allows organizations to accommodate growth while maintaining security and performance.

Finally, user education and support are vital components of a successful SAML implementation in hybrid environments. Users should be trained on how to use SSO effectively, recognize potential security threats such as phishing, and follow best practices for managing their credentials. Providing clear documentation and support channels helps users navigate any issues that arise and ensures a positive experience with the authentication system.

Handling SAML in hybrid environments requires a comprehensive approach that addresses technical, security, and user experience considerations. By implementing robust configuration, monitoring, and optimization practices, organizations can achieve seamless, secure authentication across on-premises and cloud services, enabling them to fully leverage the benefits of hybrid IT infrastructures.

Chapter 29: SAML and Multi-Factor Authentication (MFA)

In today's digital landscape, securing user authentication is more critical than ever. The growing sophistication of cyber threats, such as phishing, credential stuffing, and man-in-the-middle attacks, has exposed the vulnerabilities of traditional username-and-password authentication systems. To mitigate these risks, many organizations have turned to Multi-Factor Authentication (MFA) as an additional layer of security. When combined with Security Assertion Markup Language (SAML), MFA provides a robust framework for secure, federated identity management across diverse applications and services. This chapter explores how SAML and MFA can be integrated, the benefits of this combination, and best practices for implementation.

SAML is a widely adopted protocol that enables Single Sign-On (SSO) and federated identity management by allowing users to authenticate with a central Identity Provider (IdP) and access multiple Service Providers (SPs) without re-entering credentials. While SAML itself provides mechanisms for secure authentication through digital signatures and encryption, it does not specify how users are authenticated at the IdP level. This flexibility allows organizations to enhance SAML-based authentication by integrating MFA into the IdP's authentication process, thereby adding a critical layer of security without disrupting the user experience.

MFA enhances security by requiring users to provide two or more forms of verification before granting access. These factors typically fall into three categories: something the user knows (such as a password or PIN), something the user has (such as a smartphone or security token), and something the user is (such as a fingerprint or facial recognition). By requiring multiple forms of verification, MFA significantly reduces the likelihood of unauthorized access, even if one factor—such as a password—is compromised.

Integrating MFA into a SAML-based authentication flow involves configuring the IdP to enforce MFA policies during the authentication process. When a user attempts to access a service provider, the SP redirects the authentication request to the IdP. At this point, the IdP prompts the user to provide their primary credentials, followed by the additional MFA factors. Once the user successfully completes the MFA process, the IdP generates a SAML assertion confirming the user's identity and sends it to the SP, which grants access to the requested resource.

One of the primary benefits of integrating MFA with SAML is the ability to enforce consistent security policies across all federated applications and services. By centralizing MFA enforcement at the IdP, organizations can ensure that all service providers within the federation adhere to the same robust authentication standards. This simplifies security management, as administrators can configure and update MFA policies in a single location rather than managing them individually for each application. Additionally, users benefit from a seamless SSO experience, logging in once with MFA and gaining access to multiple services without repeated authentication prompts.

Another advantage of combining SAML with MFA is the ability to implement contextual or adaptive authentication. This approach adjusts the authentication requirements based on specific risk factors, such as the user's location, device, or behavior. For example, if a user attempts to log in from an unfamiliar location or device, the IdP can trigger additional MFA challenges to verify their identity. Conversely, if the user is accessing the service from a trusted network or device, the IdP may reduce the number of required authentication steps. This dynamic approach balances security and user convenience, providing stronger protection against potential threats while minimizing friction for legitimate users.

The flexibility of SAML allows organizations to integrate a wide range of MFA methods into their authentication processes. Common MFA methods include one-time passwords (OTPs) delivered via SMS or email, time-based one-time passwords (TOTP) generated by authenticator apps, hardware security tokens, biometric verification such as fingerprint or facial recognition, and push notifications sent to a registered device. Organizations can choose the MFA methods that best align with their security requirements, user preferences, and regulatory obligations.

When implementing SAML with MFA, it is essential to consider the user experience. While MFA adds a layer of security, it can also introduce additional steps and complexity for users. To minimize friction, organizations should adopt user-friendly MFA methods, such as push notifications or biometric authentication, which provide a quick and seamless verification process. Additionally, providing clear instructions and support for setting up and using MFA can help users adapt to the new security measures and reduce potential resistance.

Device registration and management are critical components of an effective MFA strategy. When using methods like push notifications or OTPs generated by authenticator apps, it is important to ensure that devices are securely registered and managed. This includes verifying the authenticity of devices during registration, regularly reviewing and updating registered devices, and providing mechanisms for users to report lost or compromised devices. Implementing device management policies helps maintain the integrity of the MFA process and ensures that only authorized devices are used for authentication.

Another important consideration is backup and recovery options for MFA. Users may lose access to their MFA devices due to loss, theft, or technical issues. To prevent lockouts, organizations should provide secure backup methods, such as backup codes, secondary authentication devices, or alternative verification methods. Ensuring that these backup options are both secure and accessible helps maintain user productivity while safeguarding against unauthorized access.

Integrating MFA with SAML also plays a crucial role in regulatory compliance. Many industries are subject to strict security and privacy regulations that mandate the use of strong authentication measures. For example, the General Data Protection Regulation (GDPR) in the European Union, the Health Insurance Portability and Accountability Act (HIPAA) in the healthcare sector, and the Payment Card Industry Data Security Standard (PCI DSS) in the financial industry all require robust authentication mechanisms to protect sensitive data. By implementing MFA within a SAML-based authentication framework, organizations can meet these regulatory requirements while providing secure access to critical systems and data.

Monitoring and auditing are essential for maintaining the security and integrity of SAML and MFA implementations. Organizations should log all authentication events, including successful and failed login attempts, MFA challenges, and device registrations. These logs provide valuable insights into user behavior and can help detect potential security threats, such as unauthorized access attempts or unusual login patterns. Integrating these logs with Security Information and Event Management (SIEM) solutions enables real-time monitoring, automated threat detection, and centralized incident response.

Performance considerations are also important when integrating MFA with SAML. While MFA enhances security, it can introduce latency into the authentication process, particularly if external factors like SMS delivery or push notifications are involved. To mitigate these issues, organizations should optimize their IdP infrastructure to handle MFA challenges efficiently and consider using faster MFA methods, such as TOTP or biometric verification. Ensuring that the authentication process remains responsive and reliable is crucial for maintaining a positive user experience.

Testing and validation are critical steps in deploying SAML with MFA. Organizations should thoroughly test the integration in a controlled environment to identify and resolve potential issues before rolling it out to production. This includes testing various MFA methods, verifying the handling of different user scenarios (such as device loss or network disruptions), and ensuring that the SAML assertions are correctly generated and processed. Continuous monitoring and periodic reviews help ensure that the system remains secure and performs as expected over time.

By integrating SAML with Multi-Factor Authentication, organizations can achieve a high level of security while providing a seamless and efficient authentication experience. This combination leverages the strengths of both technologies, ensuring that users can access critical applications and services securely, regardless of their location or device. Through careful planning, user-centric design, and robust security practices, organizations can effectively implement SAML and MFA to protect against evolving threats and meet the demands of today's digital landscape.

Chapter 30: Migrating to SAML from Legacy Systems

Migrating from legacy authentication systems to Security Assertion Markup Language (SAML) represents a critical step for organizations aiming to modernize their identity and access management (IAM) strategies. Legacy systems, often reliant on basic username and password authentication, present numerous challenges, including security vulnerabilities, scalability issues, and cumbersome user experiences. As organizations expand their digital ecosystems, integrating cloud services and enabling remote work, the limitations of legacy systems become increasingly apparent. SAML offers a standardized, secure, and scalable solution for federated identity management, facilitating Single Sign-On (SSO) across diverse applications and services. Successfully migrating to SAML, however, requires careful planning, strategic execution, and thorough testing to ensure a seamless transition.

The first step in migrating to SAML is conducting a comprehensive assessment of the existing authentication infrastructure. This involves identifying all systems, applications, and services currently relying on legacy authentication methods, such as LDAP-based authentication, proprietary protocols, or custom-built solutions. Understanding the scope of the migration is crucial for developing an effective strategy. It is essential to categorize applications based on their criticality, usage patterns, and compatibility with SAML. Some applications may natively support SAML integration, while others may require additional development or third-party tools to enable SAML-based authentication.

Once the assessment is complete, the next phase involves selecting and configuring a suitable Identity Provider (IdP) to serve as the central authentication authority. Popular IdP solutions include Active Directory Federation Services (ADFS), Okta, Ping Identity, and SimpleSAMLphp, among others. The choice of IdP depends on factors such as organizational size, existing infrastructure, and specific security requirements. Configuring the IdP involves defining the authentication policies, setting up user directories, and establishing trust relationships with Service Providers (SPs). This process also includes generating and managing metadata files, which contain essential information about endpoints, supported bindings, and cryptographic keys.

Data migration is another critical component of transitioning from legacy systems to SAML. This process involves transferring user credentials, attributes, and access permissions from the old system to the new IdP. It is essential to ensure that data integrity is maintained during this transfer and that sensitive information, such as passwords and personal identifiers, is securely handled. In many cases, organizations opt to synchronize their existing directories, such as Active Directory or LDAP, with the new IdP to streamline the migration process. Tools like Azure AD Connect can facilitate this synchronization, ensuring that user information remains consistent across both on-premises and cloud environments.

A key advantage of migrating to SAML is the ability to implement Single Sign-On (SSO) across multiple applications and services. SSO enhances the user experience by allowing users to authenticate once and gain access to all authorized resources without repeated logins. Implementing SSO involves configuring each SP to trust the IdP and accept SAML assertions for authentication. This requires exchanging metadata between the IdP and SP, defining attribute mappings, and ensuring that the SP correctly interprets the SAML assertions. Thorough testing is essential to verify that SSO functions as expected and that users can seamlessly access all integrated applications.

Security considerations play a pivotal role in the migration process. SAML provides robust mechanisms for securing authentication data, including digital signatures and encryption. It is crucial to configure the IdP to sign all SAML assertions, ensuring their authenticity and integrity. Additionally, sensitive user attributes should be encrypted to protect them from unauthorized access during transmission. Both the IdP and SP must support and correctly implement these security features to maintain a secure authentication environment. Regularly rotating cryptographic keys and updating metadata to reflect these changes further enhances the security posture.

While the technical aspects of migration are critical, addressing organizational and user-related factors is equally important. Migrating to SAML often involves significant changes to how users interact with authentication systems. Effective communication and training are essential to ensure that users understand the new authentication process and can navigate any changes with confidence. Providing clear instructions, support resources, and helpdesk assistance can ease the transition and minimize disruptions to productivity. Engaging stakeholders early in the migration process and incorporating their feedback can also help address potential concerns and foster acceptance of the new system.

During the migration, it is advisable to adopt a phased approach, starting with less critical applications and gradually expanding to more essential systems. This incremental strategy allows for thorough testing and troubleshooting at each stage, reducing the risk of widespread disruptions. Pilot programs can be particularly effective, enabling organizations to gather feedback, identify potential issues, and refine their implementation before rolling out SAML authentication to the entire organization. Continuous monitoring and performance assessment throughout the migration process help ensure that the new system meets security, usability, and performance expectations.

Another challenge organizations may face during migration is ensuring compatibility with applications that do not natively support SAML. In such cases, third-party tools or custom development may be required to bridge the gap. Identity brokers or federation gateways can act as intermediaries, translating SAML assertions into protocols compatible with legacy applications. This approach allows organizations to maintain access to critical systems while gradually transitioning to a fully SAML-based authentication environment. Over time, as applications are updated or replaced, these interim solutions can be phased out, further simplifying the authentication landscape.

Post-migration, it is essential to establish robust monitoring and auditing practices to maintain the security and integrity of the SAML environment. Detailed logs of authentication events, assertion processing, and user activities should be collected and analyzed to detect anomalies and potential security threats. Integrating these logs with Security Information and Event Management (SIEM) systems enables real-time monitoring, automated threat detection, and centralized incident response. Regular security assessments, vulnerability scans, and compliance audits help ensure that the SAML implementation remains secure and aligns with industry best practices and regulatory requirements.

Migrating to SAML from legacy systems is a transformative process that offers significant benefits in terms of security, scalability, and user experience. By providing a standardized framework for federated identity management and Single Sign-On, SAML enables organizations to streamline authentication across diverse applications and services. While the migration process presents technical, organizational, and security challenges, careful planning, strategic execution, and continuous improvement ensure a successful transition. As organizations embrace modern IT environments, integrating SAML into their identity and access management strategies positions them for greater flexibility, enhanced security, and improved operational efficiency.

Chapter 31: SAML in the Context of Modern Authentication

Security Assertion Markup Language (SAML) has long been a cornerstone of enterprise-level identity management, offering robust solutions for federated identity and Single Sign-On (SSO). As the landscape of authentication evolves with the advent of new technologies and protocols, SAML remains a vital player, albeit within a broader ecosystem that includes OAuth 2.0, OpenID Connect (OIDC), and other modern authentication frameworks. Understanding SAML's role in this dynamic environment is key to leveraging its strengths while integrating it seamlessly with contemporary authentication strategies.

SAML was developed in the early 2000s to address the growing need for secure, federated identity management across different domains and organizations. Its primary function is to enable users to authenticate with a central Identity Provider (IdP) and access multiple Service Providers (SPs) without needing to re-enter credentials. This federated approach to identity management has become a standard in large enterprises, educational institutions, and government organizations, where secure and efficient access to a broad range of applications is essential.

The core strength of SAML lies in its use of XML-based assertions to transmit authentication and authorization data securely. These assertions are digitally signed to ensure their integrity and authenticity, providing a high level of trust between the IdP and SP. The protocol supports robust encryption mechanisms to protect sensitive data in transit, aligning with stringent security requirements in sectors like finance, healthcare, and government. Despite these strengths, SAML's reliance on XML and complex configurations can present challenges in terms of implementation and performance, especially when compared to more lightweight protocols like OAuth 2.0 and OIDC.

As the digital landscape has shifted towards cloud computing, mobile applications, and API-driven architectures, the limitations of SAML have become more apparent. OAuth 2.0 and OIDC have emerged as popular alternatives for modern authentication needs, particularly in environments that demand flexibility, scalability, and ease of integration. OAuth 2.0, primarily designed for authorization rather than authentication, allows users to grant third-party applications limited access to their resources without sharing credentials. OIDC builds on OAuth 2.0 to provide authentication capabilities, offering a more straightforward and JSON-based approach that is well-suited for mobile and web applications.

Despite these newer protocols gaining traction, SAML continues to play a crucial role in many organizations' authentication strategies. One of the reasons for this is the extensive infrastructure and investments already made in SAML-based systems. Enterprises with established SAML IdPs and SPs may find it impractical to migrate entirely to OAuth 2.0 or OIDC, especially when SAML continues to meet their security and operational requirements effectively. Moreover, many cloud service providers, such as Microsoft Azure, Google Workspace, and AWS, support SAML alongside OAuth and OIDC, allowing organizations to maintain their existing SAML integrations while adopting newer protocols where appropriate.

In hybrid environments where both SAML and modern authentication protocols coexist, interoperability becomes a key consideration. Organizations often implement federation gateways or identity brokers that can translate between SAML and OIDC, enabling seamless integration across diverse systems. These intermediaries allow users to authenticate via SAML while accessing applications that rely on OAuth or OIDC, providing a unified and consistent authentication experience. This approach not only preserves the security and reliability of SAML but also leverages the flexibility and scalability of modern protocols.

The rise of Zero Trust architecture has further influenced the context in which SAML operates. Zero Trust emphasizes continuous verification of user identities and devices, regardless of whether they are inside or outside the traditional network perimeter. While SAML provides strong authentication mechanisms, it was originally designed with a perimeter-based security model in mind. Integrating SAML with Zero Trust frameworks requires additional considerations, such as incorporating Multi-Factor Authentication (MFA), device compliance checks, and real-time threat detection. By enhancing SAML with these modern security practices, organizations can align it with contemporary security paradigms without abandoning their existing infrastructure.

Another important factor in the modern authentication landscape is the user experience. Today's users expect seamless, fast, and intuitive access to applications, whether they are using desktop computers, mobile devices, or cloud services. SAML's reliance on browser-based redirection flows can introduce latency and complexity, particularly in mobile environments where embedded web views may not provide the best user experience. In contrast, OIDC's use of RESTful APIs and JSON Web Tokens (JWTs) offers a more streamlined approach that aligns with modern application development practices. To address this, organizations may adopt hybrid models that use SAML for traditional web applications and OIDC for mobile and API-driven applications, ensuring an optimal balance between security and usability.

Compliance with regulatory requirements also plays a significant role in the continued relevance of SAML. Many industries, such as healthcare, finance, and government, have stringent regulations regarding data security and user privacy. SAML's robust security features, including digital signatures, encryption, and detailed audit logs, help organizations meet these regulatory standards. By integrating SAML with modern compliance frameworks and ensuring that it aligns with evolving legal requirements, organizations can continue to rely on SAML as a cornerstone of their identity management strategies.

The future of SAML in the context of modern authentication will likely involve continued evolution and adaptation. While newer protocols like OIDC offer compelling advantages in terms of simplicity and flexibility, SAML's established presence, security strengths, and compatibility with enterprise systems ensure its ongoing relevance. Organizations that adopt a flexible, hybrid approach to authentication—leveraging the best features of SAML, OAuth, and OIDC—will be well-positioned to navigate the complexities of the modern digital landscape. This approach allows them to maintain robust security, ensure regulatory compliance, and deliver a seamless user experience across diverse platforms and applications.

Chapter 32: Case Studies: Real-World SAML Deployments

The real-world application of Security Assertion Markup Language (SAML) illustrates its transformative power in securing and simplifying authentication across diverse industries. By enabling Single Sign-On (SSO) and federated identity management, SAML provides organizations with a robust framework to streamline user access, reduce administrative overhead, and enhance security. The following case studies highlight how various organizations have successfully deployed SAML to meet their unique identity management needs, overcome challenges, and achieve significant operational improvements.

One of the most prominent examples of SAML deployment can be found in the education sector, where institutions often face the challenge of providing seamless access to a wide array of digital resources while maintaining stringent security protocols. The University of California system, comprising multiple campuses and thousands of students, staff, and faculty, implemented a SAML-based federation using InCommon, a higher education trust framework. Prior to adopting SAML, each campus maintained separate authentication systems, leading to fragmented user experiences and increased administrative complexity. By federating their identities through SAML, the university system enabled students and staff to access resources like digital libraries, research databases, and learning management systems with a single set of credentials. This not only improved user satisfaction but also streamlined IT operations, reducing the burden of managing multiple authentication systems and enhancing security through centralized control.

In the healthcare industry, SAML has played a critical role in enabling secure access to sensitive patient data while ensuring compliance with regulations such as the Health Insurance Portability and Accountability Act (HIPAA). A large healthcare provider in the United States faced challenges in integrating its electronic health record (EHR) systems with third-party applications, including telemedicine platforms and pharmacy management systems. By implementing SAML-based SSO, the provider allowed healthcare professionals to authenticate once and securely access multiple systems without re-entering credentials. This integration improved workflow efficiency for doctors and nurses, reduced the risk of credential fatigue, and ensured that sensitive patient information was protected through robust encryption and authentication mechanisms. Additionally, the centralized logging and auditing capabilities provided by SAML helped the organization maintain compliance with HIPAA's stringent data protection requirements.

The financial services sector has also leveraged SAML to enhance security and streamline access to critical systems. A multinational bank with operations in over 30 countries needed a solution to unify its authentication processes across various regional offices and third-party partners. Prior to SAML implementation, the bank relied on disparate legacy systems that created security vulnerabilities and complicated access management. By deploying a SAML-based federated identity system, the bank established a secure, unified authentication framework that allowed employees, contractors, and partners to access necessary resources using their existing credentials. This approach not only strengthened security by enforcing consistent authentication policies but also improved operational efficiency by reducing the need for multiple logins and simplifying user provisioning and de-provisioning processes.

In the corporate world, SAML has been instrumental in supporting the growing trend of remote work and cloud adoption. A leading technology company with a global workforce needed to integrate its on-premises Active Directory with various cloud-based applications, including Microsoft 365, Salesforce, and Slack. By implementing SAML, the company enabled employees to use their corporate credentials to access these applications securely, regardless of their location. This seamless SSO experience enhanced productivity by eliminating the need for multiple passwords and logins, while the centralized identity management provided by SAML ensured that security policies were consistently applied across all environments. The company also integrated Multi-Factor Authentication (MFA) with its SAML implementation to add an additional layer of security, protecting against phishing attacks and unauthorized access.

Government agencies, which often deal with highly sensitive data and complex security requirements, have also benefited from SAML deployments. A federal agency in charge of national cybersecurity needed to provide secure, federated access to its systems for state and local government partners. The agency implemented a SAML-based identity federation that allowed external users to authenticate using their home organizations' credentials while accessing federal systems. This approach facilitated secure inter-agency collaboration, reduced administrative overhead by eliminating the need to manage separate accounts for external users, and ensured compliance with federal security standards. The SAML deployment also included advanced auditing and monitoring capabilities, enabling the agency to track authentication events and quickly respond to potential security incidents.

In the retail industry, SAML has helped companies streamline access to a wide range of internal systems, from inventory management to customer relationship management (CRM) tools. A global retail chain with thousands of employees and stores worldwide faced challenges in managing access to its growing number of digital tools and applications. By adopting SAML-based SSO, the company enabled employees to log in once and access all necessary applications, improving efficiency and reducing the likelihood of password-related security incidents. The centralized authentication system also simplified the onboarding and offboarding processes, allowing IT teams to quickly grant or revoke access as employees joined or left the company. This not only enhanced security but also ensured that the company could scale its operations without being hindered by complex access management issues.

Educational technology providers have also successfully deployed SAML to support their platforms. A company offering online learning solutions to schools and universities needed to integrate its platform with various institutional identity providers to provide a seamless login experience for students and educators. By implementing SAML, the company enabled users to access the platform using their existing school credentials, eliminating the need for separate accounts and passwords. This integration not only improved the user experience but also enhanced data security by ensuring that authentication was handled by trusted institutional IdPs. The SAML deployment also facilitated compliance with data privacy regulations such as the General Data Protection Regulation (GDPR), as the company could rely on institutions to manage user identities and consent.

SAML has also found applications in the energy sector, where companies must secure access to critical infrastructure and sensitive data. A major utility provider implemented SAML to federate identities across its internal systems and third-party vendors. This approach allowed the company to enforce strict access controls while enabling contractors and partners to access necessary resources using their own credentials. The centralized authentication system improved security by reducing the risk of credential sharing and unauthorized access, while the detailed auditing capabilities provided visibility into who accessed what systems and when. This level of control and transparency was essential for meeting regulatory requirements and ensuring the integrity of the company's critical infrastructure.

The hospitality industry has similarly benefited from SAML deployments, particularly in managing access for a diverse workforce that includes full-time employees, part-time staff, and contractors. A large hotel chain implemented SAML to unify access to its property management systems, reservation platforms, and employee portals. By enabling SSO through SAML, the company simplified access for its staff, reduced password-related issues, and enhanced security by centralizing authentication. The SAML deployment also allowed the company to integrate with third-party service providers, such as travel agencies and loyalty programs, providing a seamless experience for both employees and customers.

These case studies demonstrate the versatility and effectiveness of SAML in addressing a wide range of identity management challenges across different industries. Whether in education, healthcare, finance, government, retail, or technology, SAML provides a robust framework for secure, federated authentication, enabling organizations to streamline access, enhance security, and improve operational efficiency. By leveraging SAML's capabilities, organizations can meet the demands of today's complex digital environments while ensuring that their identity management systems are scalable, secure, and user-friendly.

Chapter 32: Common Pitfalls and How to Avoid Them

Implementing Security Assertion Markup Language (SAML) in an organization's authentication infrastructure can significantly enhance security and streamline user access through Single Sign-On (SSO) and federated identity management. However, SAML is a complex protocol, and improper implementation can lead to security vulnerabilities, performance issues, and integration failures. Understanding the common pitfalls associated with SAML deployments and knowing how to avoid them is crucial for a successful and secure integration.

One of the most frequent mistakes in SAML implementations is improper configuration of metadata between the Identity Provider (IdP) and the Service Provider (SP). Metadata serves as the foundation of trust between the two entities, detailing endpoints, certificates, supported bindings, and other critical configuration parameters. Failing to properly exchange and validate metadata can lead to authentication failures, with the SP rejecting assertions or the IdP not recognizing authentication requests. To avoid this, organizations should ensure that metadata is accurately configured, regularly updated, and securely exchanged. Metadata should be signed to ensure its authenticity, and both parties should verify that all information, such as entity IDs and endpoint URLs, matches the expected values.

Another common pitfall is neglecting to properly manage cryptographic keys used for signing and encrypting SAML assertions. Digital signatures are essential for ensuring the integrity and authenticity of SAML messages, while encryption protects sensitive information from unauthorized access. Using weak encryption algorithms, failing to rotate keys regularly, or mishandling key storage can expose the system to security risks. Organizations should adopt strong cryptographic algorithms like RSA with SHA-256 or ECDSA, securely store private keys in hardware security modules (HSMs), and implement key rotation policies to minimize the risk of key compromise. It's also essential to ensure that the corresponding public keys are correctly shared through metadata and that both the IdP and SP validate signatures rigorously.

Time synchronization issues between the IdP and SP are another frequent source of SAML failures. SAML assertions include time-sensitive conditions, such as NotBefore and NotOnOrAfter timestamps, which define the validity period of the assertion. If the clocks on the IdP and SP are out of sync, assertions may be rejected as expired or not yet valid, leading to failed authentications. To prevent this, both systems should synchronize their clocks using a reliable Network Time Protocol (NTP) server. Regular monitoring and verification of time settings across all servers involved in the SAML flow help maintain consistency and prevent time-related errors.

Attribute mapping errors can also disrupt SAML integrations. SAML assertions often carry user attributes that the SP uses to provision accounts, assign roles, or enforce access controls. Inconsistent attribute naming conventions, mismatched data formats, or missing attributes can result in users being denied access or granted inappropriate permissions. To avoid these issues, organizations should clearly define the required attributes and their formats in the metadata and ensure that the IdP is configured to release the correct attributes. Testing the attribute flow using SAML tracing tools can help identify discrepancies and ensure that the SP receives the necessary information in the expected format.

Binding mismatches between the IdP and SP can cause communication failures during the SAML authentication process. SAML supports multiple bindings, such as HTTP Redirect, HTTP POST, and HTTP Artifact, each with specific implementation requirements. If the IdP and SP are configured to use different bindings or if the binding is improperly implemented, authentication requests and responses may fail. To mitigate this, organizations should verify that both entities support and are configured to use the same bindings. Thorough testing of each binding method in various scenarios can help ensure compatibility and identify potential issues before deployment.

Single Logout (SLO) implementation can be particularly challenging in SAML environments. SLO allows users to terminate sessions across all connected applications with a single logout action, but inconsistent support for SLO among different SPs and IdPs can result in partial logouts or lingering sessions. This can pose a security risk, as users may assume they are fully logged out when sessions remain active in some applications. To address this, organizations should ensure that all SPs and IdPs involved in the federation support SLO and are correctly configured to handle logout requests and responses. Testing the SLO process thoroughly helps identify gaps and ensures that sessions are properly terminated across the board.

Another pitfall is failing to secure SAML assertions adequately. While digital signatures protect the integrity of assertions, sensitive data within the assertions can still be exposed if not properly encrypted. Assertions often contain personally identifiable information (PII), such as email addresses, usernames, and group memberships, which could be exploited if intercepted. Organizations should encrypt sensitive attributes within the SAML assertion and ensure that assertions are transmitted over secure channels using Transport Layer Security (TLS). Additionally, SPs should validate the audience restriction conditions in assertions to ensure they are intended for the correct recipient.

Ignoring the importance of comprehensive logging and monitoring is another common oversight in SAML implementations. Without detailed logs, diagnosing issues, tracking user activity, and identifying potential security breaches becomes challenging. Organizations should enable detailed logging on both the IdP and SP to capture authentication events, assertion processing, and error messages. These logs provide valuable insights into the system's behavior and can help identify the root cause of issues. Integrating logs with Security Information and Event Management (SIEM) solutions enables real-time monitoring and automated threat detection, enhancing the organization's overall security posture.

Performance issues can also arise if SAML implementations are not optimized for scalability and efficiency. The XML-based nature of SAML assertions and the computational demands of cryptographic operations can introduce latency, particularly in high-traffic environments. Organizations should implement caching mechanisms for metadata and session tokens to reduce processing overhead and improve response times. Load balancing and high-availability configurations help distribute authentication requests evenly and ensure that the system can handle increased traffic without performance degradation.

Neglecting to conduct thorough testing before deploying SAML integrations into production is a critical mistake that can lead to unexpected failures and security vulnerabilities. Organizations should establish comprehensive testing protocols that cover various scenarios, including successful and failed authentications, different user roles, SLO processes, and edge cases like expired certificates or network disruptions. Using SAML tracing tools and automated testing frameworks helps identify potential issues early and ensures that the system behaves as expected under different conditions.

Lack of proper user training and support can also hinder the success of SAML implementations. Users may be unfamiliar with SSO processes or encounter difficulties with new authentication methods, leading to frustration and increased support requests. Providing clear documentation, training sessions, and responsive support channels helps users adapt to the new system and ensures a smooth transition. Educating users about the importance of security practices, such as recognizing phishing attempts and safeguarding their credentials, further enhances the overall security of the SAML environment.

Failure to establish clear governance policies for managing federated identities can result in inconsistent security practices and administrative confusion. In federated environments involving multiple organizations, it is essential to define roles, responsibilities, and procedures for managing trust relationships, metadata exchanges, and security incidents. Regular reviews and audits of federated partnerships help maintain alignment with security standards and ensure that all entities adhere to agreed-upon policies.

By understanding these common pitfalls and proactively addressing them, organizations can ensure the success and security of their SAML implementations. Careful planning, thorough testing, robust security practices, and continuous monitoring are essential components of a resilient and efficient SAML-based authentication infrastructure. Through diligent attention to detail and adherence to best practices, organizations can leverage SAML to provide secure, seamless access to critical applications and services.

Chapter 33: Extending SAML with Custom Attributes

Security Assertion Markup Language (SAML) is a powerful protocol used for enabling Single Sign-On (SSO) and federated identity management across a wide range of applications and services. One of its key strengths lies in its ability to transmit user information securely between an Identity Provider (IdP) and a Service Provider (SP) through SAML assertions. While SAML defines a standard set of attributes, many organizations find it necessary to extend these assertions with custom attributes to meet specific business requirements, improve user experience, and enhance security. Extending SAML with custom attributes allows organizations to tailor authentication and authorization processes to their unique needs, providing more granular control over user access and enabling richer user interactions.

Custom attributes in SAML assertions serve to provide additional information about a user beyond the standard attributes like name, email, or role. These attributes can include department codes, security clearance levels, project assignments, or any other data relevant to the organization's operations. By including custom attributes, organizations can implement fine-grained access control policies, ensuring that users have access to resources based on detailed criteria that go beyond basic identity verification. This level of customization is particularly valuable in complex environments where access decisions depend on multiple factors, such as organizational hierarchy, geographic location, or compliance requirements.

The process of extending SAML with custom attributes begins at the Identity Provider, where the user's identity is authenticated, and the SAML assertion is generated. The IdP must be configured to retrieve the necessary custom attributes from the user directory, such as Active Directory, LDAP, or a custom database. This often involves mapping directory attributes to SAML attributes, ensuring that the correct data is included in the assertion. For example, if an organization wants to include a user's department in the SAML assertion, the IdP configuration must map the department field from the directory to a SAML attribute, such as "department" or a custom-defined name.

Once the IdP is configured to include custom attributes in the SAML assertions, the Service Provider must be able to interpret and utilize these attributes effectively. This requires configuring the SP to recognize the custom attributes and apply them to access control policies, user provisioning processes, or application-specific logic. For instance, a content management system might use a custom "clearanceLevel" attribute to determine which documents a user can access, or a project management tool might use a "projectCode" attribute to filter tasks and resources relevant to the user's assigned projects.

One of the challenges in extending SAML with custom attributes is ensuring consistency and interoperability between the IdP and SP. Both parties must agree on the naming conventions, data formats, and usage of custom attributes to avoid misinterpretation or errors in the authentication process. It is essential to document the custom attributes thoroughly, including their names, data types, and intended use, and to share this documentation with all stakeholders involved in the SAML integration. This collaborative approach helps prevent issues where an SP fails to recognize a custom attribute or applies it incorrectly due to inconsistent configurations.

Security is a critical consideration when extending SAML with custom attributes. Since SAML assertions may contain sensitive information, such as user roles, permissions, or personal data, it is essential to protect these attributes from unauthorized access and tampering. All SAML assertions should be digitally signed to ensure their integrity and authenticity, and sensitive attributes should be encrypted to protect them during transmission. Additionally, the Service Provider should validate the SAML assertions rigorously, checking the digital signature, verifying the issuer, and ensuring that the assertions are intended for the correct audience.

Another important aspect of managing custom attributes in SAML is controlling attribute release policies. The Identity Provider should only release the minimum necessary attributes required by the Service Provider to perform its functions. This principle of data minimization helps protect user privacy and reduces the risk of data leakage. Organizations should carefully review and define which attributes are shared with each Service Provider, ensuring that sensitive information is only disclosed when absolutely necessary. Implementing granular attribute release policies allows organizations to strike a balance between providing sufficient information for application functionality and maintaining robust privacy protections.

Performance considerations also come into play when extending SAML with custom attributes. Including too many attributes in a SAML assertion can increase the size of the assertion and slow down the authentication process, particularly in environments with high user volumes or complex attribute sets. To mitigate this, organizations should optimize the attribute selection process, focusing on the most critical attributes needed for access decisions and application functionality. Regularly reviewing and refining the attribute set can help maintain efficient performance while ensuring that all necessary information is included in the assertions.

Testing and validation are essential steps in the process of extending SAML with custom attributes. Organizations should thoroughly test the SAML assertions to ensure that custom attributes are correctly included, formatted, and interpreted by the Service Providers. This involves using SAML tracing tools to capture and inspect the assertions, verifying that the attributes are present and accurate, and confirming that the Service Providers apply them correctly in their access control and user provisioning processes. Continuous monitoring and periodic audits help maintain the integrity of the SAML integration and ensure that custom attributes continue to meet the organization's evolving needs.

Extending SAML with custom attributes also provides opportunities for integrating SAML with other identity and access management (IAM) solutions. For example, custom attributes can be used to synchronize user information between SAML and directory services, such as LDAP or Active Directory, or to integrate with role-based access control (RBAC) systems. By leveraging custom attributes, organizations can create a cohesive IAM ecosystem that supports comprehensive access management policies, dynamic user provisioning, and seamless interoperability across diverse applications and services.

In complex environments, organizations may also encounter the need to transform or manipulate custom attributes before including them in SAML assertions. This can involve formatting data to meet specific application requirements, combining multiple directory fields into a single attribute, or applying conditional logic based on user roles or group memberships. Identity Providers often support scripting or policy frameworks that allow administrators to define these transformations, providing greater flexibility in how custom attributes are generated and applied. By leveraging these capabilities, organizations can tailor their SAML assertions to meet the precise needs of their applications and business processes.

As organizations continue to evolve and adopt new technologies, the ability to extend SAML with custom attributes remains a powerful tool for adapting identity management to meet changing requirements. Whether supporting complex access control policies, integrating with diverse applications, or enhancing user experiences, custom attributes provide the flexibility and granularity needed to manage identities effectively in today's dynamic digital landscape. By following best practices for attribute management, security, and interoperability, organizations can ensure that their SAML implementations remain robust, secure, and responsive to their unique needs.

Chapter 34: The Future of SAML and Identity Standards

Security Assertion Markup Language (SAML) has long been a cornerstone of federated identity management, enabling Single Sign-On (SSO) and secure authentication across a wide range of applications and organizations. Introduced in the early 2000s, SAML provided a standardized method for exchanging authentication and authorization data between identity providers (IdPs) and service providers (SPs), addressing critical needs in enterprise security and user convenience. However, as the digital landscape evolves with the rise of cloud computing, mobile applications, and API-driven architectures, the future of SAML and identity standards is being shaped by new technologies, protocols, and security paradigms.

The continued relevance of SAML in modern identity management is closely tied to its widespread adoption in enterprise environments. Many large organizations have built extensive infrastructures around SAML, integrating it into their internal applications, cloud services, and partner ecosystems. This entrenched presence means that SAML is unlikely to disappear in the near future, even as newer protocols like OAuth 2.0 and OpenID Connect (OIDC) gain traction. Instead, SAML is expected to coexist with these modern protocols, forming part of a hybrid identity management strategy that leverages the strengths of each standard.

One of the key factors influencing the future of SAML is the growing emphasis on user experience and developer-friendly technologies. SAML's reliance on XML and complex configurations can be challenging for developers, especially when compared to the simplicity and flexibility of JSON-based protocols like OIDC. As organizations seek to streamline development processes and improve user experiences, there is a clear trend toward adopting more lightweight and API-friendly authentication methods. However, the robust security features and proven reliability of SAML continue to make it a preferred choice for many high-security environments, such as government agencies, financial institutions, and large enterprises.

The rise of Zero Trust security models is also reshaping the landscape of identity standards, including SAML. Zero Trust principles emphasize continuous verification of user identities and strict access controls, regardless of the user's location or network. While SAML provides strong authentication mechanisms, it was originally designed for a perimeter-based security model, where trust is established at the network boundary. Integrating SAML into Zero Trust frameworks requires additional layers of security, such as Multi-Factor Authentication (MFA), contextual access policies, and real-time threat detection. As organizations adopt Zero Trust architectures, SAML implementations will need to evolve to support these dynamic and adaptive security requirements.

Interoperability between SAML and modern protocols is another area of focus for the future of identity standards. Many organizations operate in hybrid environments where SAML-based systems coexist with OAuth 2.0 and OIDC applications. To facilitate seamless integration, identity federation gateways and brokers are being used to translate authentication flows between different protocols. This approach allows organizations to maintain their existing SAML infrastructure while embracing the flexibility and scalability of modern authentication standards. As these interoperability solutions mature, they will play a critical role in enabling unified identity management across diverse platforms and ecosystems.

Cloud computing has had a profound impact on the evolution of identity standards, and SAML's role in cloud environments continues to be significant. Many cloud service providers, such as Microsoft Azure, Google Workspace, and AWS, support SAML for federated authentication, allowing organizations to extend their on-premises identity systems to the cloud. However, the dynamic nature of cloud applications and the increasing reliance on APIs have driven the adoption of OAuth 2.0 and OIDC as more suitable standards for certain use cases. The future of SAML in cloud environments will likely involve continued support for legacy applications and high-security use cases, while newer applications and services adopt more modern protocols.

The proliferation of mobile devices and the demand for seamless mobile authentication experiences have also influenced the trajectory of identity standards. SAML's browser-based redirection flows can introduce challenges in mobile environments, where embedded web views and native applications require more streamlined authentication mechanisms. OIDC, with its support for RESTful APIs and JSON Web Tokens (JWTs), offers a more mobile-friendly approach that aligns with modern application development practices. While SAML may remain a viable option for certain enterprise and web-based applications, the shift toward mobile-first development will likely drive increased adoption of OIDC in the coming years.

As the field of identity management continues to evolve, privacy and regulatory compliance remain critical considerations. SAML's robust security features, including digital signatures, encryption, and detailed audit logs, help organizations meet stringent data protection requirements such as the General Data Protection Regulation (GDPR) and the Health Insurance Portability and Accountability Act (HIPAA). However, as privacy regulations become more complex and global in scope, identity standards will need to adapt to ensure compliance. This may involve enhanced data minimization techniques, improved consent management frameworks, and more granular control over attribute sharing in federated identity environments.

Decentralized identity is an emerging concept that has the potential to influence the future of identity standards, including SAML. Decentralized identity models, such as those based on blockchain technology and self-sovereign identity (SSI) principles, aim to give individuals greater control over their personal data and digital identities. These models challenge the traditional centralized approach of identity providers and service providers by enabling peer-to-peer authentication and verification. While SAML's centralized federation model may not align directly with decentralized identity principles, there is potential for hybrid approaches that incorporate elements of both models to enhance privacy, security, and user autonomy.

The evolution of SAML and identity standards will also be shaped by advancements in artificial intelligence (AI) and machine learning. These technologies offer new opportunities for enhancing authentication processes, detecting anomalies, and preventing fraud. By integrating AI-driven analytics with identity management systems, organizations can implement more adaptive and intelligent authentication mechanisms that respond to evolving threats in real time. While SAML provides the foundational framework for secure authentication, the incorporation of AI technologies will add an additional layer of sophistication to identity verification and access control.

As organizations continue to navigate the complexities of digital transformation, the future of SAML and identity standards will be defined by the need for flexibility, security, and interoperability. While newer protocols like OAuth 2.0 and OIDC offer compelling advantages in terms of simplicity and adaptability, SAML's established presence, robust security features, and compatibility with enterprise systems ensure its ongoing relevance. By adopting a holistic approach that leverages the strengths of multiple identity standards, organizations can create resilient and scalable identity management solutions that meet the demands of modern digital ecosystems.

Chapter 35: Comparing SAML 2.0 with OAuth and OpenID Connect

As organizations increasingly adopt digital solutions, the need for secure and efficient authentication protocols has grown significantly. Security Assertion Markup Language (SAML) 2.0, OAuth 2.0, and OpenID Connect (OIDC) are three of the most widely used protocols for managing authentication and authorization. While they serve overlapping purposes, each has unique characteristics, strengths, and limitations. Understanding the differences between these protocols is essential for selecting the right solution based on an organization's specific requirements, whether that involves enterprise-level Single Sign-On (SSO), API security, or modern web and mobile application authentication.

SAML 2.0, introduced in 2005, was designed to provide federated identity management and enable Single Sign-On across different domains. It allows users to authenticate once with a trusted Identity Provider (IdP) and access multiple Service Providers (SPs) without re-entering credentials. SAML uses XML-based assertions to transmit authentication and authorization information securely between the IdP and SP. This protocol is highly structured and supports robust security mechanisms, such as digital signatures and encryption, to ensure the integrity and confidentiality of the authentication process. SAML's design makes it particularly well-suited for enterprise environments, educational institutions, and government agencies that require strong security and centralized control over user identities.

OAuth 2.0, released in 2012, addresses a different aspect of the authentication landscape. It is primarily an authorization framework rather than an authentication protocol. OAuth allows users to grant third-party applications limited access to their resources without sharing their credentials. This is achieved through the issuance of access tokens, which applications use to access protected resources on behalf of the user. OAuth's focus on authorization makes it ideal for securing APIs and enabling third-party integrations, such as allowing a social media app to post content on a user's behalf without requiring the user's password. OAuth is more flexible and lightweight than SAML, utilizing JSON for data representation and supporting various grant types to accommodate different use cases, including web, mobile, and server-to-server communication.

OpenID Connect, built on top of OAuth 2.0, extends the authorization capabilities of OAuth to include authentication. By adding an identity layer to the OAuth framework, OIDC allows applications to verify the identity of users and obtain basic profile information. OIDC uses JSON Web Tokens (JWTs) to transmit identity information securely, making it a more developer-friendly and modern approach to authentication. OIDC supports RESTful APIs and integrates seamlessly with mobile and web applications, offering a streamlined user experience and easier implementation compared to SAML. Its widespread adoption by major technology providers, such as Google and Microsoft, has further cemented its position as a leading standard for modern authentication.

One of the most significant differences between SAML and OAuth/OIDC lies in their data formats and protocols. SAML relies on XML, which is verbose and can be more complex to parse and handle, especially in environments where performance and efficiency are critical. In contrast, OAuth and OIDC use JSON, a lightweight and widely supported data format that is easier to work with in modern application development. This difference makes OAuth and OIDC more suitable for mobile and web applications, where performance and ease of integration are paramount.

The user experience also varies between these protocols. SAML typically involves browser-based redirection flows, where the user is redirected to the IdP for authentication and then back to the SP with a SAML assertion. This process can introduce latency and is less suited to mobile environments, where embedded web views and native applications require more streamlined authentication mechanisms. OIDC, with its support for API-based authentication and flexible token handling, provides a smoother user experience, particularly in mobile and single-page applications (SPAs). OAuth's token-based approach also allows for more granular control over access permissions, enabling features like token expiration and scope-limited access, which are not natively supported in SAML.

Security is a critical consideration when comparing these protocols. SAML provides robust security features, including digital signatures, encryption, and detailed assertion validation. Its mature security model makes it a trusted choice for environments that require high levels of security and compliance, such as financial institutions and government agencies. OAuth and OIDC, while secure, rely on the correct implementation of security best practices, such as secure token storage and proper handling of redirect URIs. The flexibility of OAuth can introduce vulnerabilities if not implemented correctly, such as token leakage or insufficient validation of authorization codes. However, when implemented properly, OAuth and OIDC provide strong security suitable for a wide range of applications.

Interoperability is another factor to consider. SAML is well-established in enterprise environments, with broad support across enterprise applications and services. Many legacy systems and enterprise platforms are built around SAML, making it the default choice for organizations with existing SAML infrastructure. OAuth and OIDC, on the other hand, are better suited for modern applications and cloud-based services. Their lightweight, flexible design makes them easier to integrate with contemporary development frameworks and APIs. As organizations increasingly adopt hybrid environments that combine on-premises and cloud-based applications, the need for interoperability between SAML and OAuth/OIDC has grown. Federation gateways and identity brokers can facilitate this interoperability, allowing organizations to leverage the strengths of each protocol while maintaining a cohesive identity management strategy.

Scalability and performance are important considerations in large-scale deployments. SAML's XML-based assertions and complex processing can introduce performance overhead, particularly in high-traffic environments. OAuth and OIDC, with their JSON-based tokens and streamlined protocols, offer better performance and scalability, especially in API-driven and mobile-centric architectures. The ability to handle stateless authentication with JWTs further enhances the scalability of OIDC, reducing the need for server-side session management and improving response times.

Another aspect to consider is the ecosystem and community support surrounding each protocol. SAML, being older and more established, has a wealth of documentation, tools, and best practices available for enterprises. However, its complexity can be a barrier to entry for developers new to identity management. OAuth and OIDC benefit from a vibrant developer community and extensive support from major technology providers, making them more accessible for modern application developers. The availability of libraries, SDKs, and comprehensive documentation simplifies the implementation process, allowing developers to focus on building secure and user-friendly applications.

In terms of future-proofing identity management strategies, the choice between SAML, OAuth, and OIDC depends on the specific needs and goals of the organization. SAML's robust security and entrenched presence in enterprise environments ensure its continued relevance for traditional applications and high-security use cases. However, the flexibility, performance, and ease of integration offered by OAuth and OIDC make them the preferred choice for modern applications, cloud services, and API security. Organizations may find that a hybrid approach, leveraging SAML for legacy systems and OIDC for new applications, provides the best balance of security, usability, and future readiness.

Ultimately, the decision to use SAML, OAuth, or OIDC should be guided by the specific requirements of the application, the existing infrastructure, and the desired user experience. By understanding the strengths and limitations of each protocol, organizations can implement a secure, efficient, and scalable identity management solution that meets the evolving demands of the digital landscape.

Chapter 35: Legal and Compliance Considerations in SAML

Security Assertion Markup Language (SAML) has become a foundational protocol for enabling Single Sign-On (SSO) and federated identity management across a wide range of industries and organizations. While SAML provides robust security mechanisms for authentication and authorization, its implementation also carries significant legal and compliance implications. These considerations are critical for ensuring that identity management systems align with regulatory requirements, protect user privacy, and mitigate legal risks associated with data handling and security breaches. Understanding the legal and compliance landscape surrounding SAML is essential for organizations that rely on this protocol to manage sensitive user information and facilitate secure access to applications and services.

One of the primary legal considerations in SAML implementations is compliance with data protection and privacy regulations. Regulations such as the General Data Protection Regulation (GDPR) in the European Union, the Health Insurance Portability and Accountability Act (HIPAA) in the United States, and the California Consumer Privacy Act (CCPA) impose strict requirements on how personal data is collected, processed, and shared. SAML assertions often contain personally identifiable information (PII), such as names, email addresses, and group memberships, which are subject to these regulatory frameworks. Organizations must ensure that their SAML implementations handle this data in a manner that complies with applicable laws, including obtaining appropriate user consent, minimizing data collection, and implementing robust security measures to protect the information.

GDPR, in particular, has far-reaching implications for SAML deployments, especially for organizations that operate across international borders. Under GDPR, personal data must be processed lawfully, transparently, and for a specific purpose. SAML implementations must therefore include mechanisms for informing users about how their data will be used and obtaining explicit consent where required. Additionally, GDPR mandates that personal data should only be shared with third parties if there is a legal basis for doing so, and appropriate safeguards must be in place to protect the data during transmission and storage. This means that organizations using SAML for federated identity management must carefully evaluate their data-sharing practices and ensure that Service Providers (SPs) adhere to the same high standards of data protection.

HIPAA introduces another layer of compliance requirements for organizations in the healthcare sector. HIPAA mandates the protection of Protected Health Information (PHI) and establishes strict guidelines for data privacy, security, and breach notification. When SAML is used to authenticate access to healthcare applications or systems that handle PHI, organizations must ensure that SAML assertions are transmitted securely, with appropriate encryption and access controls in place. Additionally, HIPAA requires detailed audit trails and logging of access events, which means that SAML implementations must include comprehensive logging capabilities to track authentication activities and detect unauthorized access attempts.

The CCPA, which applies to businesses operating in California or handling the personal data of California residents, imposes requirements related to data transparency, user rights, and security. SAML implementations must facilitate compliance with CCPA by enabling organizations to provide users with access to their personal data, honor requests for data deletion, and implement security measures to protect against data breaches. This includes ensuring that SAML assertions are handled securely, that data minimization principles are applied, and that users are informed about how their data is shared within federated identity ecosystems.

Beyond these specific regulations, SAML implementations must also consider broader legal principles related to data security and breach liability. Data breaches involving SAML assertions or authentication systems can expose organizations to significant legal and financial risks, including regulatory fines, legal actions, and reputational damage. To mitigate these risks, organizations must implement robust security practices, such as using strong encryption algorithms, regularly rotating cryptographic keys, and conducting regular security assessments of their SAML infrastructure. Additionally, organizations should establish incident response plans that outline procedures for detecting, reporting, and mitigating data breaches involving SAML systems.

The contractual relationships between Identity Providers and Service Providers in a federated identity environment also carry legal implications. Organizations must establish clear agreements that define the roles and responsibilities of each party, including how user data will be handled, what security measures will be implemented, and how compliance with legal requirements will be ensured. These agreements should address issues such as data ownership, liability for data breaches, and procedures for responding to security incidents. By formalizing these arrangements through legally binding contracts, organizations can protect themselves from legal disputes and ensure that all parties are held accountable for maintaining data security and compliance.

Cross-border data transfers present another complex legal challenge for SAML implementations, particularly in federated environments involving international partners. Different countries have varying data protection laws, and transferring personal data across borders can trigger additional legal requirements. For example, under GDPR, transferring personal data outside the European Economic Area (EEA) requires that appropriate safeguards, such as Standard Contractual Clauses (SCCs) or Binding Corporate Rules (BCRs), are in place. Organizations must carefully assess the legal frameworks governing cross-border data transfers and ensure that their SAML implementations comply with these requirements to avoid legal exposure.

In addition to regulatory compliance, SAML implementations must address industry-specific standards and certifications that govern data security and identity management. For example, organizations in the payment card industry must comply with the Payment Card Industry Data Security Standard (PCI DSS), which mandates strict security controls for handling cardholder data. SAML implementations in this context must ensure that authentication processes meet PCI DSS requirements, including the use of strong encryption, secure transmission protocols, and detailed logging of access events. Similarly, organizations seeking certifications such as ISO 27001 or SOC 2 must demonstrate that their SAML implementations adhere to the security and privacy controls required by these standards.

User consent and transparency are also critical components of legal compliance in SAML implementations. Organizations must ensure that users are informed about how their data will be used and shared within federated identity systems. This includes providing clear privacy notices, obtaining explicit consent where required, and offering users the ability to manage their data preferences. Transparency in data handling practices not only supports legal compliance but also builds trust with users, demonstrating the organization's commitment to protecting their privacy and security.

Data minimization and purpose limitation are key principles in many data protection regulations and should be integral to SAML implementations. Organizations should only include the minimum necessary attributes in SAML assertions required to perform authentication and authorization functions. This reduces the risk of unnecessary data exposure and ensures that personal information is only used for its intended purpose. Regular audits and reviews of attribute release policies can help organizations maintain compliance with data minimization principles and identify opportunities to further reduce data collection and sharing.

Auditability and accountability are essential for demonstrating compliance with legal and regulatory requirements. SAML implementations must include comprehensive logging and monitoring capabilities to track authentication events, detect anomalies, and provide evidence of compliance. These logs should capture details such as login attempts, assertion processing, and attribute sharing activities, and should be securely stored and regularly reviewed. In the event of a security incident or regulatory audit, having detailed, tamper-proof logs can help organizations respond effectively and demonstrate their commitment to data protection and compliance.

Legal and compliance considerations in SAML implementations are multifaceted and require a thorough understanding of the regulatory landscape, industry standards, and best practices for data security and privacy. By proactively addressing these considerations, organizations can ensure that their SAML deployments not only provide secure and efficient identity management but also align with legal requirements and mitigate the risks associated with data breaches and non-compliance. Through robust security practices, clear contractual agreements, and a commitment to transparency and user rights, organizations can navigate the complex legal landscape surrounding SAML and maintain the trust of their users and stakeholders.

Chapter 36: SAML Community and Resources

The Security Assertion Markup Language (SAML) has established itself as a cornerstone of federated identity management and Single Sign-On (SSO) systems across various industries, from education to healthcare to large-scale enterprise environments. A protocol that enables secure, standardized communication of authentication and authorization data between Identity Providers (IdPs) and Service Providers (SPs), SAML has grown not only through formal specifications but also through a vibrant, global community of developers, security professionals, and organizations dedicated to its implementation and evolution. Understanding and leveraging the SAML community and the myriad resources it offers can significantly enhance the implementation, security, and ongoing management of SAML-based systems.

The SAML community is broad and diverse, encompassing contributors from academia, private enterprise, open-source initiatives, and government institutions. At its foundation is the OASIS (Organization for the Advancement of Structured Information Standards) consortium, the body responsible for the development and maintenance of the SAML standard. OASIS provides the formal specifications, ensuring the protocol remains consistent, interoperable, and secure across implementations. The consortium's commitment to transparency and collaboration has made it a trusted authority in the realm of identity standards, fostering an environment where feedback from the community can influence the direction of future updates.

Beyond OASIS, numerous open-source projects and commercial vendors have contributed significantly to the SAML ecosystem. Tools like Shibboleth, SimpleSAMLphp, and OpenSAML have become widely adopted, offering robust, flexible frameworks for implementing SAML in various contexts. Shibboleth, in particular, has been instrumental in higher education, where institutions require federated access to shared resources like research databases and academic platforms. SimpleSAMLphp, a lightweight and easy-to-configure PHP-based implementation, has become a go-to solution for developers looking to integrate SAML with web applications quickly. These projects are not only maintained by dedicated teams but also benefit from active community contributions, where users share bug fixes, enhancements, and best practices through forums, mailing lists, and repositories.

Community-driven forums and discussion groups play a pivotal role in the dissemination of knowledge and support within the SAML ecosystem. Platforms like Stack Overflow, GitHub, and specialized mailing lists provide spaces where developers can seek advice, troubleshoot issues, and share experiences related to SAML implementations. The collaborative nature of these platforms ensures that even niche problems can find solutions, often drawing from the collective expertise of a global network of practitioners. Discussions often cover a wide range of topics, from basic configuration questions to complex security considerations, reflecting the diverse needs and challenges faced by those working with SAML.

In addition to forums, comprehensive documentation and educational resources are critical components of the SAML community. The official OASIS specifications provide in-depth technical details, but for many practitioners, more accessible guides and tutorials are invaluable. Resources like the Shibboleth documentation, SimpleSAMLphp guides, and numerous online tutorials offer step-by-step instructions for configuring and deploying SAML systems. These resources often include practical examples, code snippets, and troubleshooting tips, making them essential for both beginners and experienced professionals. Moreover, many educational institutions and professional organizations offer training programs and certifications focused on identity management and SAML, providing structured learning paths for those seeking to deepen their expertise.

Security is a paramount concern within the SAML community, and numerous resources are dedicated to addressing the evolving threat landscape. Best practices for securing SAML implementations are widely shared through whitepapers, blog posts, and conference presentations. Topics such as preventing XML Signature Wrapping (XSW) attacks, securing metadata exchanges, and implementing robust key management practices are commonly discussed, reflecting the community's commitment to maintaining the integrity and security of SAML systems. Security-focused conferences and workshops, such as Identiverse and the Internet2 Global Summit, provide platforms for professionals to share the latest research, tools, and strategies related to SAML and broader identity management topics.

The role of federations in the SAML community cannot be overstated. Federations like InCommon in the United States, eduGAIN in Europe, and others around the world provide frameworks for trust and interoperability among participating institutions. These federations establish policies, governance structures, and technical standards that ensure consistent and secure SAML implementations across member organizations. By participating in federations, organizations benefit from a trusted network of partners, streamlined access to shared resources, and support structures that facilitate compliance with legal and regulatory requirements.

The SAML community also benefits from ongoing innovation and the integration of SAML with other identity standards and technologies. As hybrid environments become more common, with organizations leveraging both SAML and newer protocols like OAuth 2.0 and OpenID Connect (OIDC), resources that address interoperability and integration challenges are increasingly valuable. Identity brokers and federation gateways are frequently discussed within the community, offering solutions for bridging different protocols and creating cohesive identity management systems. The exchange of knowledge and tools related to these integrations highlights the community's adaptability and its focus on meeting the evolving needs of modern IT environments.

Another vital aspect of the SAML community is the emphasis on real-world case studies and shared experiences. Organizations often publish detailed accounts of their SAML implementation journeys, outlining challenges faced, solutions devised, and lessons learned. These case studies provide practical insights that go beyond theoretical knowledge, offering valuable guidance for others embarking on similar projects. Whether it's a university federating access to research resources, a healthcare provider securing patient data, or a multinational corporation streamlining employee access across global offices, these stories illustrate the diverse applications and benefits of SAML.

The future of the SAML community is closely tied to the broader evolution of identity and access management (IAM). As new technologies and standards emerge, the community remains a critical resource for ensuring that SAML continues to meet the demands of modern security and interoperability. Continuous contributions from developers, researchers, and organizations help keep the protocol relevant, secure, and aligned with best practices. The open, collaborative nature of the SAML community ensures that it remains a dynamic and supportive environment for anyone involved in identity management.

In essence, the strength of the SAML community lies in its diversity, collaboration, and commitment to excellence. By engaging with this community and leveraging its vast resources, organizations can not only implement SAML effectively but also stay ahead of emerging challenges and opportunities in the ever-evolving field of identity management. Whether through formal specifications, open-source projects, forums, or federations, the SAML community provides the knowledge, tools, and support needed to build secure, scalable, and interoperable identity systems.

Chapter 37: Final Thoughts and Next Steps

The journey through understanding and implementing Security Assertion Markup Language (SAML) highlights both its complexities and its immense potential in modern identity management. As a foundational protocol for federated identity and Single Sign-On (SSO), SAML has played a pivotal role in shaping how organizations handle secure authentication and authorization. From its robust security features to its ability to integrate with a diverse range of applications and services, SAML continues to be a trusted standard in enterprise environments, government institutions, and educational sectors.

As organizations increasingly adopt hybrid environments, combining on-premises infrastructure with cloud-based applications, the role of SAML remains significant, albeit within a more complex ecosystem. The evolution of identity standards has brought forth protocols like OAuth 2.0 and OpenID Connect (OIDC), each offering unique advantages in specific contexts, such as API security and mobile application authentication. However, the coexistence of these protocols with SAML reflects the broader trend of adopting multi-layered identity management strategies that leverage the strengths of various standards to meet evolving security, usability, and regulatory requirements.

The future of identity management is being shaped by emerging technologies and paradigms, including Zero Trust security models, decentralized identity frameworks, and the growing integration of artificial intelligence in cybersecurity. SAML's adaptability will be key to maintaining its relevance in this rapidly changing landscape. Organizations can enhance their SAML implementations by integrating them with Multi-Factor Authentication (MFA), contextual access controls, and real-time monitoring tools, ensuring that they align with the latest security best practices while continuing to deliver seamless user experiences.

For those embarking on SAML implementations, the journey begins with understanding the protocol's architecture, core concepts, and security considerations. Setting up a simple SAML environment involves configuring Identity Providers and Service Providers, establishing trust relationships through metadata exchange, and ensuring that assertions are properly signed and encrypted. As implementations grow more complex, advanced configuration techniques become essential, including fine-tuning attribute release policies, optimizing performance, and integrating with third-party applications and cloud services.

Troubleshooting SAML errors is an inevitable part of the process, given the protocol's complexity and the variety of environments it operates within. Understanding common pitfalls, such as misconfigured metadata, time synchronization issues, and attribute mapping errors, is crucial for maintaining a stable and secure SAML deployment. Tools like SAML tracers, logging systems, and security information and event management (SIEM) platforms play a vital role in identifying and resolving issues, ensuring that authentication flows remain smooth and reliable.

Legal and compliance considerations are also integral to successful SAML deployments. With regulations like GDPR, HIPAA, and CCPA imposing strict requirements on data handling and privacy, organizations must ensure that their SAML systems are configured to protect personal data and maintain detailed audit logs. Cross-border data transfers, contractual agreements between federated partners, and adherence to industry-specific standards all require careful attention to mitigate legal risks and ensure compliance with applicable laws.

As SAML continues to evolve, the community of developers, administrators, and security professionals dedicated to advancing the protocol plays a crucial role in its growth and refinement. Open-source projects, industry consortia, and professional networks provide valuable resources for learning, troubleshooting, and staying informed about the latest developments in SAML and identity management. Participating in this community not only enhances technical knowledge but also fosters collaboration and innovation, helping organizations navigate the complexities of modern identity systems.

Looking ahead, the next steps for organizations and individuals involved in SAML implementations involve continuous learning and adaptation. The identity landscape is dynamic, with new threats, technologies, and regulatory requirements emerging regularly. Staying informed about these changes, conducting regular security assessments, and updating SAML configurations accordingly are essential practices for maintaining robust and secure identity management systems. Additionally, exploring integrations with newer protocols like OIDC, adopting Zero Trust principles, and considering the potential of decentralized identity models will position organizations to meet the future challenges of identity and access management.

Ultimately, SAML's enduring value lies in its ability to provide secure, scalable, and interoperable solutions for federated identity management. By understanding its capabilities, addressing its challenges, and integrating it within a broader identity strategy, organizations can harness the full potential of SAML to protect their digital assets, streamline user experiences, and support their mission in an increasingly connected world.

www.ingramcontent.com/pod-product-compliance
Lightning Source LLC
LaVergne TN
LVHW051238050326
832903LV00028B/2458